CLOSE THE COALHOUSE DOOR

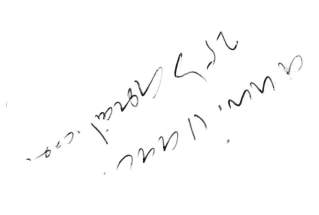

FROM STORIES BY SID CHAPLIN

Close the Coalhouse Door

A STAGE PLAY IN THREE ACTS BY

ALAN PLATER

WITH SONGS BY ALEX GLASGOW

BLOODAXE BOOKS

ISBN: 978 1 85224 489 7

New version first published 2000 by
Bloodaxe Books Ltd,
Eastburn,
South Park,
Hexham,
Northumberland NE46 1BS.

Reprinted 2014

Original version published 1969 by Methuen.

www.bloodaxebooks.com
For further information about Bloodaxe titles
please visit our website or write to
the above address for a catalogue.

Supported using public funding by
ARTS COUNCIL
ENGLAND

Printed in Great Britain by Bell & Bain Limited, Glasgow, Scotland, on
acid-free paper sourced from mills with FSC chain of custody certification.

ORIGINAL VERSION

Close the Coalhouse Door was first presented at the Newcastle Playhouse on 9 April 1968 with the following cast:

WILL JOBLING	Kevin Stoney
THOMAS MILBURN	Colin Douglas
EXPERT	Dudley Foster
MARY ANN MILBURN	Brenda Peters
VICAR	Robin Parkinson
JACKIE	John Woodvine
GEORDIE	Bryan Pringle
JOHN MILBURN	Alan Browning
FRANK MILBURN	Ralph Watson
RUTH	Geraldine Moffatt
SINGING PITWOMAN	Jean Becke
OTHER GUESTS	Catherine Brandon
	James Garbutt
	Fred Pearson
	Colin Hale
	Elayne Sharling
	Helen Stephenson
MUSICIANS	Bill Southgate (*musical director*)
	Jerry Rochefort (*drums*)
	and members of the Craghead Colliery Band
DIRECTOR	Bill Hays
MUSICAL DIRECTION	Bill Southgate
SETTING & LIGHTING DESIGN	Brian Currah

The Newcastle production transferred to the Nottingham Playhouse on 7 October 1968 and to the Fortune Theatre, London, on 22 October 1968.

NEW VERSION

The new version of *Close the Coalhouse Door* was first presented by the Live Theatre Company at Live Theatre, Newcastle, on 1 October 1994, with the following cast:

THOMAS MILBURN	Donald McBride
EXPERT / VICAR	Gez Casey
MARY ANN MILBURN	Charlie Hardwick
JACKIE	David Whitaker
GEORDIE	Trevor Fox
JOHN MILBURN	Joe Caffrey
FRANK MILBURN	Tony Neilson
RUTH	Libby Davison

Other parts were played by members of the company

DIRECTOR	Max Roberts
MUSICAL DIRECTION	Ieuan Goch ab Einion
DESIGNER	Nigel Hook
TECHNICAL MANAGER	Perry Hudson
STAGE MANAGERS	Mel Creighton, Richard Stadius
WARDROBE	Joanne Salter
SCENIC ARTIST	Roger Wood
ADDITIONAL MUSIC	Hetton Silver Band

ACT ONE

Darkness. The song begins and as it continues the lights go up to show the pithead and the slag-heap behind, grey but not without poetry. A solo voice, off-stage.

SONG. Close the coalhouse door, lad,
　　　There's blood inside.
　　　Blood from broken hands and feet
　　　Blood that's dried on pit-black meat
　　　Blood from hearts that know no beat
　　　Close the coalhouse door, lad,
　　　There's blood inside.

The song ends. A moment's silence then an electric bell rings, harshly. JACKIE walks into a pool of light near the pithead.

JACKIE. Divven' fret, Tommy lad, I can hear ye.

JACKIE sets the winding gear in motion and the cage comes up to the surface – indicated by the noise of the machinery and lights fading up on the cage, with THOMAS MILBURN inside. He opens the gate and steps out.

JACKIE. Are you all right, Tommy?

THOMAS. Aye, I'm all right.

JACKIE. Like it's the big day today, isn't it?

THOMAS. Aye, it's the big day all right.

The EXPERT walks into a spotlight at the opposite side of the stage.

EXPERT. Just one moment, please. You're probably wondering who these men are and what they are doing. Well, first of all, the year is 1968.

THOMAS. I remember 1968 like it was yesterday.

JACKIE. Aye, and you know what a bloody awful day it was yesterday.

EXPERT. Do you mind? I'm very busy here with a historical context.

THOMAS. Carry on, pet.

EXPERT. The year is 1968 and this is a disused coalmine in the village of Brockenback... (*Long 'o'.*)

THOMAS. Brockenback. (*Sharply, with short 'o'.*)

EXPERT. Brockenback. (*A good try.*) However, this mine is linked by underground workings to the large, modern coalmine at Datton, five miles away. It is necessary to keep this shaft at ...Brockenback open simply to keep the pumps in operation so as to avoid the danger of flooding at Datton. The pumping machinery is in the capable hands of these two gentlemen.

Pause.

Right. From the top of the cage, I mean the top of the page.

THOMAS *and* JACKIE *resume their conversation.*

THOMAS. What's it to be? Double or quits or a fresh game?

JACKIE. Double or quits.

THOMAS. Serves you right.

THOMAS *tosses two pennies in the air. They look eagerly to see how they fall. Obviously an old ritual.*

THOMAS. Two tails.

JACKIE. Ye bugger!

JACKIE *pays up.*

EXPERT. What you have just seen is a simplified version of the old traditional coalminers' pastime known as pitch and toss. Please regard me as your friend, ladies and gentlemen ... available throughout the evening to explain these sociological nuances, sort out problems of translation and ...

THOMAS. (*Sharply.*) Hadaway to hell!

EXPERT. 'Hadaway to hell.' This is a vernacular expression equivalent to the Cockney 'sling your hook' or...

THOMAS. (*Breaks in.*) Hadaway to hell!

JACKIE. And take your historical nuances with you.

EXPERT *"exits"– though this is a technicality because what he actually does is a quick change into the* VICAR *and crosses to the Party set.*

THOMAS. Anyhow, you're all ready for the party?

JACKIE. Certainly I am. I'll not miss your party, Tommy. I mean, it's not every day you have a golden wedding, is it?

THOMAS. Aye, it's not every day.

THOMAS *exits.* JACKIE *walks us into the party. Those present:* MARY ANNE MILBURN, *the* VICAR, GEORDIE *and whoever else we can muster – including, by implication, the audience.*

VICAR. Where's the blushing bridegroom, Mrs Milburn?

MARY. He's out the back washing hisself...

VICAR. Cleanliness is next to Godliness, you know...

MARY. Aye, I never could see that, myself...

GEORDIE *steps forward.*

GEORDIE. Cleanliness, you say? You ought to meet wor lass. Oh, she's a disgusting woman, a disgusting woman. Every time I want a piddle, the sink's full of dirty dishes.

JACKIE. Is she not here tonight?

GEORDIE. She's on the late turn. She helps her Dad in his black-smith shop.

JACKIE. What does she do?

GEORDIE. She hands him the horses.

JACKIE. Hey, hold your tongue, Geordie, you'll get us chucked out...

MARY. Why, speak of the devil...

As THOMAS *enters, all spick and span.*

MARY. Where've you been all this time?

THOMAS. Been getting washed, woman, what do you think?

MARY. I think you've been out the back playing pitch and toss.

THOMAS. Would I do a thing like that, did you ever?

He crosses to JACKIE *and* GEORDIE, *taking out his coins as he does so.*

THOMAS. Wotcheor lads, are you ready?

As they start the game, the VICAR *talks to* MARY.

VICAR. Don't worry, Mrs Milburn, it's been going on for generations.

MARY. I know. We've got a letter from the Co-op bank manager to prove it.

VICAR. There was a Methodist preacher gave a famous sermon about pitch and toss...

MARY. Getaway.

VICAR. Over a hundred years ago.

MARY. Nothing changes.

Rapid lighting change so that the VICAR *is in a dramatic solo spot and the group of men playing pitch and toss are in semi-silhouette. Quiet chords on a church organ and the men acting out the sermon as it unfolds.*

VICAR. (*Old-style Methodist.*) And as I walked in the street I beheld only stillness, and heard naught but the singing of birds. So I lifted mine eyes unto the hills and there I beheld a multitude. I came closer unto the multitude and may I now bear witness to what I saw upon the hillside. I beheld men of faith. In the beginning, they raised their heads and looked upwards toward Heaven with cries of 'Oh God!'...

The men look up.

VICAR. ...And then they cast their eyes downward in deep humility with cries of 'Oh Christ!'...

The men look down as the coins fall.

VICAR. Among some, there was great rejoicing, while others fell silent...and then let forth great shouts, invoking the name of the Lord.

The lights revert to normal. The MEN, *who have been silent throughout the sequence, let rip with their reactions to the game, ad lib, carrying us into the action of the present.*

JACKIE. You lucky bugger, Geordie...

GEORDIE. Never mind that, let's see your money...

GEORDIE *collects up money then crosses to the audience.*

GEORDIE. It's real money we're using, you know. All legal tender. (*Throws notes to audience.*) Green Shield stamps. There you are, pet. Treat yourself to a carriage clock.

JACKIE. Hey, where's your John, he likes a game?

THOMAS. He's in bed.

MARY. Working nights, he'll be down soon.

GEORDIE. What about young Frank?

A slight pause, a hint of tension.

THOMAS. We'll not see him.

VICAR. Frank's your other grandson, isn't he?

MARY. Yes...and he'll be here, he wrote and said he would.

THOMAS. He's wrote letters before...

MARY. He's a busy lad.

THOMAS. Aye, and I'm a busy lad an' all... 'course it's a long way, all the way from Newcastle...

MARY. Oh, hold your tongue, man...

VICAR. Perhaps I shouldn't have asked.

THOMAS. She thinks the sun shines out of wor Frank's...

VICAR. Amen.

MARY. That'll do. He was clever enough to stay out of the pit... and you'll not forgive anybody that...

JACKIE. Howay, Tommy, don't let's be fighting...

GEORDIE. Why, what's a happy family without a bit of fighting?

VICAR. There's probably something in that.

GEORDIE. I mean, take my mother-in-law...please...

JACKIE. Go on...we can tell there's more...

GEORDIE. (*To audience.*) She's a terrible woman, my mother-in-law, a terrible woman. Been with us fourteen years, she has, fourteen terrible years...mind you, it's her house.

MARY. Frank'll turn up, you'll see.

THOMAS. I'll give you five to one against...and look you, there's no takers...

MARY. I remember a feller giving five to one against the King marrying Mrs Simpson...

THOMAS. Anyhow, shut up about Frank, I want to enjoy myself.

As JOHN *enters.*

JOHN. Talking about Frank, are we?

THOMAS. No, we're not.

JOHN. Good.

MARY. That'll do. He is your brother.

JOHN. Aye, some say...

JACKIE. Working tonight, are you, John lad?

JOHN. Later on... like a treat to look forward to.

THOMAS. Why, he doesn't know he's bloody born.

JACKIE. Aye, that's true.

JOHN. I'll swap you your job any day, Mr Union man.

THOMAS. Gans off to work in his motor car...

GEORDIE. Like a merchant banker...

JOHN. Tell us a merchant banker gans off to work in the middle of the night.

JACKIE. You're getting well paid, lad.

JOHN. I know that...'Cause I'm worth it.

THOMAS. Listen to the lad.

JACKIE. I wonder what Tommy Hepburn would say, hearing him talk like that.

JOHN. Who's Tommy Hepburn?

GEORDIE. Who's Tommy Hepburn, did you ever!

JOHN. Is it the cocky feller plays left-half for Sunderland?

THOMAS. He knows bonny well who he is.

JACKIE. Your first Trade Union leader, that's who he is.

MARY. Now they're off.

JACKIE. It was Tommy Hepburn formed the first union that covered the two counties.

A lighting change.

14

JOHN. And what did he do when he'd formed it?

JACKIE. Why, man, what do you think he did? He called a bloody strike, what else?

A beating drum.

JACKIE. March 21st, 1831, and twenty thousand miners assemble on the Town Moor to hear Thomas Hepburn speak.

In the following sequence the part of HEPBURN *is played by* JACKIE, *the* PITMEN *by* THOMAS *and* GEORDIE, *the* PITMAN'S WIFE *by* MARY.

HEPBURN. I am not here to make a speech. I want you people to tell the meeting in your own words what your grievances are. Mr Charlton...

As FIRST PITMAN *steps forward.*

CHARLTON. I just want pay for the work I do. Instead of giving it all back to the owners.

HEPBURN. How do you give it back to the owners, Mr Charlton?

CHARLTON. I fill my corve with coal. There's supposed to be seven and a half hundredweight of coal in it ... if it's two pounds under weight, I don't get paid ... if there's four pounds of stones in it, I don't get paid.

HEPBURN. Four pounds out of seven and a half hundredweight.

CHARLTON. That's right. I filled eight corves yesterday. I got paid for one... but then I got fined for not working hard enough so I ended up paying the owners.

HEPBURN. What light do you have to work by in the mine, Mr Charlton?

CHARLTON. One candle.

HEPBURN. Mr Robson...

SECOND PITMAN *steps forward.*

ROBSON. My grievance is that I want to be paid in money...

HEPBURN. In money?

ROBSON. Every penny I get has to be spent at the Tommy shop...

HEPBURN. That's the shop that belongs to the mine owners?

ROBSON. That's right. And if there's any money owing to the shop, they deduct it from my pay... and now they've started paying us with tokens that have to be spent at the Tommy shop...

HEPBURN. And what happens if you complain about this?

ROBSON. They throw you out of your house... because your house belongs to the owners as well...

HEPBURN. Mrs Mather.

PITMAN'S WIFE *steps forward.*

MATHER. I want to know why my son should work eighteen hours a day down the pit. He gans down when it's dark, he comes up when it's dark... seven days a week...when's he going to see the sunshine?

HEPBURN. When does he go to school, Mrs Mather?

MATHER. What school?

HEPBURN. How old is your son, Mrs Mather?

MATHER. He's six years old, Mr Hepburn.

HEPBURN *addresses the meeting.*

HEPBURN. Lads, you know the reason for all this. We are all victims of the Bond...that piece of paper we sign once a year, agreeing to work for the owners on their terms. And you've heard what their terms mean.

Reactions.

Lads, you will be asked to sign your next annual bond on April 5th. We will refuse, each and every one of us, until the owners meet our demands.

Reactions.

We are demanding a twelve-hour working day for boys. We are demanding that our wages be paid in money, and that we be free to spend that money wherever we please.

Reactions.

The men of each colliery will meet twice a week, each colliery to send a delegate to a central committee. Each of us will subscribe sixpence so we can send petitioners to Parliament, to plead our case. All in favour of these resolutions?

Unanimous show of hands.

Lads... to know how to wait is the secret of success. The time will come when the golden chain that binds the tyrants together will be snapped: when men will be properly organised; when coal owners will be like ordinary men and will have to sigh for the days gone by.

The lights revert to normal.

JOHN. (*Sceptical.*) And what happened?

THOMAS. There was a great strike in 1831, another one in 1832.

JOHN. Aye, but what happened?

THOMAS. Oh, the coal owners called in the military, there was a lot of fighting, a couple of murders.

JACKIE. That's when they hanged Will Jobling. Accused of murdering a magistrate. Found guilty, naturally. And they displayed his body on a gibbet on Jarrow Slake as an example to the proletariat.

THOMAS. The last man to be hung on a gibbet in this country. A collier from Jarrow.

JACKIE. That's what I call a historical nuance.

JOHN. And what did it all achieve?

JACKIE. The owners agreed a twelve-hour day for boys of six years old.

GEORDIE. And the conscience of the nation was stirred, never forget that.

JOHN. All agreed on paper?

JACKIE. Don't be daft, man, they never agreed anything on paper... the Union wasn't recognised.

THOMAS. We had to take the word of the coal owners...

JACKIE. As aristocrats and gentlemen.

Pause.

THOMAS. Aye.

GEORDIE. Aye.

JACKIE. Aye.

THOMAS. That really was a Union. It's all different now.

JACKIE. That's true enough.

GEORDIE. (*To* JACKIE.) I bet you know a song about it.

JACKIE. I wouldn't be at all surprised.

And JACKIE *sings his song.*

> When that I was and a little tiny boy,
> Me daddy said to me,
> 'The time has come, me bonny bonny bairn
> To learn your ABC.'
> Now Daddy was a Lodge Chairman
> In the coalfields of the Tyne
> And his ABC was different
> From the Enid Blyton kind.
> He sang...

Possible wheeze is that members of the cast join in with JACKIE *in shouting the letters as he comes to them, but it's essentially a solo number.*

JACKIE. (*Sings.*)
> A is for Alienation that made me the man that I am,
> And B's for the Boss who's a bastard, a bourgeois who don't give a damn.
> C is for Capitalism, the boss's reactionary creed,
> And D's for Dictatorship, laddie, but the best proletarian breed.
> E is for Exploitation that the workers have suffered so long,
> And F is for Old Ludwig Feuerbach,

GEORDIE. Who?

JACKIE. The first one to see it was wrong.
> G is for all Gerrymanders like Lord Muck and Sir Whatsisname,
> And H is the Hell that they'll go to, when the workers have kindled the flame.
> I is for Imperialism and America's kind is the worst,
> And J is for sweet Jingoism that the Tories all think of the first.
> K is for good old Keir Hardie who fought out the working-class fight,
> And L is for Vladimir Lenin, who showed him the Left was all right.
> M is of course for Karl Marx the daddy and mammy of them all,

18

And N is for Nationalisation, without it we'd crumble and fall.
O is for Over-production that capitalist economy brings,
And P is for all Private property – the greatest of all of the sins.
Q is for Quid pro quo that we'll deal out so well and so soon,
When R for Revolution is shouted,

ALL. And the Red Flag becomes the top tune!

JACKIE. S is for sad Stalinism that gave us all such a bad name,
And T is for Trotsky the hero, who had to take all of the blame.
U's for the Union of workers, the Union will stand to the end,
And V is for Victimisation, when you find out who's really your friend.
W's for all Willing workers, and that's where the memory fades,
For X Y and Z, me dear daddy said, will be written on the street barricades.
But now that I'm not a little tiny boy
Me daddy says to me,
'Please try to forget the things I said,
Especially the ABC.'
For Daddy's no longer a Union man,
And he's had to change his plea.
His alphabet is different now,
Since they made him a Labour MP.

FRANK *and* RUTH *enter towards the end of the song. They join the on-stage applause and then the others realise they have arrived.*

MARY. Frank, pet...

MARY *and* FRANK *embrace.*

FRANK. Hello, Grandma...

THOMAS. Condescended to come, then...

FRANK. Did you think I wouldn't?

JOHN. You wouldn't dare stay away.

FRANK. There you are, Granda...Johnny Walker's golden best.
And those are for you, Grandma...

He gives THOMAS *a bottle of whisky,* MARY *a bunch of flowers.*

THOMAS. Ta. (*Almost grateful.*)

MARY. Thanks you very much. I'd rather have the Scotch, mind.

THOMAS. We'll negotiate a settlement.

FRANK. You're looking fit, John.

JOHN. It's all the sunshine and fresh air I get down the pit. You're looking very pale yourself.

FRANK. Late nights and drinking out of wet glasses in Gosforth.

He introduces RUTH, *who looks a slightly alien element in this context.*

FRANK. This is Ruth... my grandmother...

MARY. Hello, pet.

FRANK. My brother, John.

RUTH. Hello, John.

JOHN. Hello, Ruth.

FRANK. My grandfather...

THOMAS. Grandfather? Did you ever... hello, pet.

RUTH. Nice to meet you, I've heard a lot about you.

MARY. It's all true.

THOMAS. You're courting, are you, you two?

FRANK. You might say.

RUTH. Sort of.

THOMAS. Sort of! I always knew if I was bloody well courting.

MARY. Getaway. I had to give you a book of instructions.

GEORDIE. My father used to say to me, 'Never get married, lad, and bring your children up the same way.'

JACKIE. You are at the college as well, are you, pet?

VICAR. And what are you reading at University?

GEORDIE. I thought you had to be able to read before they'd let you in?

RUTH. Postgraduate research, the same as Frank.

GEORDIE. Sounds dirty to me.

MARY. Everything sounds dirty to you.

GEORDIE. Never you mind, I've heard a few things about New-castle...Jesmond Road especially. That's where they all wear mink coats and no knickers...

MARY. Pay no attention to him, I'm glad you both came...

FRANK. I bet they've all been having a good crack.

MARY. They never stop.

FRANK. Tommy Hepburn?

JOHN. What do you know about Tommy Hepburn?

FRANK. Well, him and the other Union leaders, they fought for education for the miners...he gave me my chance, didn't he?

JOHN. He missed me, didn't he?

THOMAS. You're getting educated at the coal face, that's the best education of all.

JOHN. Anyways, who wants to talk about ancient history, what's the matter with football and dogs...?

GEORDIE. Did I tell you, Joe Pattinson's got hisself a new dog?

JACKIE. Oh, aye, what sort?

GEORDIE. He says it's an African whippet...

JACKIE. An African whippet?

GEORDIE. I says to him, it looks a bit fierce, Joe...yes, he says, it's been like that since we cut his mane off.

JOHN. See? Nothing changes. Not even the jokes.

GEORDIE. I had my own greyhound once, you know. Canny dog, but slow. Never won a race. So in the end I took it to a field and walked away from it.

FRANK. (*To* JACKIE.) So you've done Tommy Hepburn? What about Martin Jude?

JOHN. Martin who?

FRANK. He led the 1844 strike.

JOHN. Getaway.

THOMAS. The Great Strike.

JOHN. Not another bloody strike.

FRANK. Another bloody strike, yes.

JOHN. All them strikes just to get my little brother some education?

And a moment of tension between the brothers.

RUTH. Pack it in, the two of you! Anybody'd think you were brothers.

MARY. Good lass.

JOHN. (*To* RUTH.) Your business, is it?

RUTH. That's for me to decide.

JOHN. A woman who thinks for herself? It'll never catch on. I think I'll open that bottle of whisky you brought, young Frank.

JOHN *picks up the bottle, moves away.*

A roll of drums and a lighting change.

In the strike sequence, all the parts are played by those onstage, with simple costume changes – a hat, a coat, a cloak, shawls and scarves.

VICAR. Strike meeting, Shadon's Hill, 1844, forty thousand men present. Their leader, Mr Martin Jude.

THOMAS *as* MARTIN JUDE.

JUDE. If we have come to the field of battle, let us fight nobly and the day will be ours.

A persistent drumbeat under JUDE'S *speech, leading into the song to come.*

All the employers think about is getting as much work done for as little pay as possible and when they are not able to go any further, they turn us out of doors. Brothers, the employers want to reduce our wages. Do we agree to this?

A shout of 'No!'

They think we are ignorant. Well, if we are ignorant, what is the cause? Have those who profit from our labours done anything towards our education? What school accommodation was ever provided for workers' children? The owners sink a shaft and build hovels for workmen to live in. Those who have children are housed on the same principle as those who have none. I know of families with seven and eight children grown up to men and women in one small space... four yards by five yards... the miner's home and castle...

The song starts, in chorus.

ALL. Time for to make a stand, me lads,
Time for to take a hand, me lads,
Time for us to unite, me lads,
Time for to start a fight, me lads.
Time, Time, Time,
Time for to get the pitman some justice and peace.

JUDE. (*Speaks over music link, instrumental only.*) Brothers, it's
time to say to the Lords and Masters, we want paying for
the work we do, a fair rate, not a penny less, and no more
cheating by the managers.

ALL. Time for to make a stand, me lads,
Time for to take a hand, me lads,
Time for us to unite, me lads,
Time for to start a fight, me lads,
Time, Time, Time,
Time for to get the pitman some justice and peace.

JUDE. Brothers, it is time to say, this is the end of our slavery, this
is the end of our bondage.

ALL. Time for to make a stand, me lads,
Time for to take a hand, me lads,
Time for us to unite, me lads,
Time for to start a fight, me lads,
Time, Time, Time,
Time for to get the pitman some justice and peace.

JUDE. Brothers, I ask you to stand faithfully by your Union. I ask
you to separate from this meeting in a peaceable manner. And
I beg you, at all times keep the peace or you will smash the
Union.

MARY, *in top hat, as* LORD LONDONDERRY.

LONDONDERRY. Of course, this is all very moving but you must
realise there are two sides to this question.

JACKIE. Lord Londonderry, coal owner and gentleman...

LONDONDERRY. The most deluded and obstinate victims of design-
ing men must now perceive that they cannot become masters
and dictate terms to the coal owners. Sensible men have left
the Union and returned to work. Pitmen, I enjoin! I conjure

you to look upon the ruin you are bringing on your wives, your children, your county and your country. I gave you two weeks to consider whether you would return to work before I proceeded to eject you from your houses. I found you dogged, obstinate and determined... indifferent to my really paternal advice and kind feelings.

VICAR.   The Epistle of St James, Chapter Five. Go to now, ye rich men, weep and howl for the miseries that shall come upon you.

LONDONDERRY.   I was bound to act up to my word, bound by duty to my property, my family and my station.

VICAR.   Your silver and gold is cankered; and the rust of them shall be a witness against you and shall consume your flesh as it were fire.

LONDONDERRY.   I have now brought forty Irishmen to the pits, and if, by the thirteenth of the month, a large body of pitmen do not return to their labour, I will obtain one hundred more, and proceed to eject that number, who are now illegally and unjustly in the possession of my houses, and in the following week a further one hundred shall follow.

Fade out light on LONDONDERRY *so that the stage is in darkness. There is a loud hammering. Fade up lights on the house which is now a pitman's house of the period. In it a* PITMAN *and his* WIFE, *played by* FRANK *and* RUTH, *are sleeping. The hammering is repeated and the lights go up to reveal a* POLICEMAN, *a* BAILIFF, *a* SOLDIER. *The* PITMAN *gets up and opens the door. The* POLICEMAN *comes in, the others follow.*

POLICEMAN.   Will you gan to work?

The PITMAN *looks round the room.*

Will you gan to work?

He looks at his WIFE, *who looks away.*

For the third time. Will you gan to work?

Pause.

JUDE.   (*From the darkness, a voice.*) I beg you, at all times, to keep the peace or you will smash the Union.

PITMAN.   No.

24

The eviction proceeds. All the furniture – what there is – is carried outside, where it is deposited roughly. The WIFE *carries the baby.*

Outside, the PITMAN *arranges the furniture in a rough square, then throws a canvas sheet over the top to keep out the rain. He and his wife and child huddle beneath it. As the eviction nears completion there is a slow handclapping from neighbours, augmented by pots and pans, which reaches a rapid, deafening climax. Then stops with a sudden bang. Silence.*

Out of the silence:

VICAR. Ye have lived in pleasure on the earth and been wanton; ye have nourished your hearts as in the day of slaughter; ye have condemned and killed the just; and he doth not resist you.

LONDONDERRY. Believe me, I am your sincere friend, Lord Londonderry.

JUDE. Thirty-five thousand men, women and children were evicted in Northumberland and Durham during the 1844 strike.

LONDONDERRY. Your sincere friend.

VICAR. Be patient therefore, brethren, unto the coming of the Lord.

JACKIE. After twenty weeks on strike the following resolution was carried at meetings throughout the two counties.

JUDE. Seeing the present state of things, and being compelled to retreat from the field through the overbearing cruelty of our employers, the suffering of our families, and the treachery of those who have been at work during the strike, we at the present time deem it necessary to make the best terms with the employers we can. Agreed?

Slowly the hands go up.

It is resolved that no single individual shall go to the colliery office for work, but that all shall go in a body and meet the resident viewer. Agreed?

Again the hands go up. A group of miners cross the stage and meet LONDONDERRY *and his* MANAGER.

MANAGER. Now, lads, I suppose you request an interview with me?

They nod, almost imperceptibly.

25

MANAGER. I know what conclusion you have come to. You mean to commence on the employers' terms. Well... things will be just the same as they were before you left work... just the same...

The men look up and there is a spark of rebellion, but silent.

JUDE. (*Off.*) I beg you at all times, keep the peace, or you will smash the Union.

MANAGER. Just the same.

A pause, then the MANAGER *turns and goes off, the men following.* LONDONDERRY *watches, smiling, then follows them.*

A light on the PITMAN'S WIFE. *She no longer has the baby.*

She sings. The men sing 'Time for to make a stand' as a counter-melody.

WIFE. Twenty long weeks, twenty long weeks,
Bonny black bird, twenty long weeks,
Singin' that song, like nothin' was wrong,
Haven't you heard? Twenty long weeks.

Twenty long weeks, twenty long weeks,
Canny black bird, twenty long weeks,
Yon soft feathered breast, may warm the bairns' nest
But my bairn lies dead; twenty long weeks.

Twenty long weeks, twenty long weeks,
Fly away high, twenty long weeks,
But birdie take care, there's hawks in the air,
And not only there; twenty long weeks.

By the end of the song, the stage is in darkness except for a light on the WIFE. *This fades out as the lights fade up on the party scene, still bright but thoughtful now.*

JACKIE. There's never been a strike like that one.

MARY. You sound sorry about it.

JACKIE. No, I'm not sorry. There was over much suffering...

GEORDIE. There was plenty that died.

THOMAS. Plenty.

MARY. My granda was in it...

RUTH. Your grandfather was in it?

26

THOMAS. She's even older than she looks.

MARY. It might be history to some people. To us it's family, pet.

JACKIE. What happened to him?

MARY. He was a Union man... he was blacklisted.

FRANK. I thought there was no victimisation.

JACKIE. They always *say* that.

MARY. He went on the parish.

GEORDIE. So this woman come knocking at me door, says we're taking a collection for the workhouse, hev you got owt for us? Why, aye, I says, wait there, I'll gan and fetch wor lass...

VICAR. They brought in a lot of Welsh and Irish didn't they? In the strike?

THOMAS. Hundreds.

VICAR. What happened to them?

THOMAS. Most of them went home again... like gentle reason prevailed...

He brandishes a clenched fist by way of explanation.

JACKIE. They were shown the error of their ways...

VICAR. But no victimisation?

THOMAS. Persuasion, that's all, Vicar... friendly persuasion...

GEORDIE. Some of them turned the other cheek and had to be persuaded twice.

RUTH. (*To* FRANK.) Are they always like this?

FRANK. Like what?

RUTH. Living in the past?

THOMAS. What's the matter with the lass?

MARY. She wants to know if you always live in the past.

GEORDIE. The past, it's the best place. Especially if you're a Sunderland supporter. Besides, what's posterity ever done for me?

THOMAS. And don't forget, we've had a bigger ration of past here than most places...

JACKIE. And there's great traditions.

RUTH. You could make new traditions...

JACKIE. If you're talking about building for the future, I agree with you, but you've got to study the past first... pick the teams... see who's on your side... and who isn't.

RUTH. You're still fighting Lord Londonderry?

JACKIE. Aye, he keeps changing his name but...

THOMAS. Anyways, don't go asking a pitman to think about tomorrow...

RUTH. Why not?

THOMAS. Because, pet,... it doesn't always arrive.

JOHN. All the same, she's dead right.

FRANK. Is she really?

JOHN. Yes, she is... really.

FRANK. How do you mean?

JOHN. What I mean is, I'm sick of all the stories about the pitmen getting a good hiding.... Tell us a story where the pitmen won, for God's sake...

JACKIE. They won in 1872.

THOMAS. That's right.

A light change.

JACKIE. On August 10th, 1872 the Coal Mines Regulation Bill became law.

As the men speak, we hear quiet drumbeats building up to the single chorus at the end of the sequence. MARY *as* FIRST PITMAN, GEORDIE *as* SECOND PITMAN.

FIRST PITMAN. No boy under the age of ten, and no girl or woman of any age shall be employed in any coalmine.

ALL. Time for to make a stand, me lads.

SECOND PITMAN. Boys of the age of ten shall not be employed in any mine unless such labour be necessary by reason of the thinness of the seam.

28

ALL. Time for to take a hand, me lads.

FIRST PITMAN. The boy shall not work more than six hours in the day, and not more than six days in any one week... if he works less than six days in the week, he may work up to ten hours in any one day...

ALL. Time for us to unite, me lads.

SECOND PITMAN. Boys aged between twelve and sixteen shall work below ground not more than fifty-four hours in a week and not more than ten hours in any one day.

ALL. Time for to start a fight, lads.

FIRST PITMAN. Boys aged twelve and thirteen shall attend school at least twenty hours in a fortnight, Sundays not being included.

ALL. Time...

SECOND PITMAN. The system of working mines with single shafts is abolished.

ALL. Time...

FIRST PITMAN. All coal shall be paid for by weight instead of by measure.

ALL. Time...

SECOND PITMAN. The owners shall make returns of all coal raised yearly out of their mines, and also a return of all lives lost, and all personal injury sustained by explosion, inundations or accidents of whatever nature.

ALL. Time for to get the pitman some justice and peace.

Pause.

FIRST PITMAN. In this way Parliament recognised all the main grievances of the Miners' Unions.

THOMAS. Like Tommy Hepburn said... forty years previous... to know how to wait is the secret of success.

And a lighting link back into the present but less abrupt than previous links – the two are more or less as one till the end of the Act.

VICAR. It was a long time to wait, forty years...

FRANK. And then for what?

JACKIE. A thirty-six-hour week for lads of ten…a fifty-four-hour week for lads of twelve…

FRANK. You see what I mean?

JACKIE. We'd got something down on paper, Frank lad, and that had never happened before…

THOMAS. And the rulers of the land had listened to the working man, and that had never happened before…

GEORDIE. And we'd stirred the conscience of the Nation, and that had never happened before…well, hardly ever…

RUTH. What about Lord Londonderry?

JACKIE. Still there.

GEORDIE. I mean, the way I look at it is, like it wasn't the end, or even the beginning of the middle of the end, or even the start of the beginning of the middle of the end…but…

JACKIE. Gan on…

GEORDIE. More like the start of the middle of the beginning.

JACKIE. Only not in so many words.

THOMAS. And Tommy Hepburn, the lad that started it, he died the year after the Mines Bill was passed…and he died a pauper…

JACKIE. But he'd seen what he was fighting for come to pass.

VICAR. After forty years.

JACKIE. It was a long forty years for Tommy.

THOMAS. It was forty long years for everybody.

GEORDIE. Howay, this is supposed to be a fifty-year celebration not a forty-year wake!

THOMAS. Aye, but it's a grand old story. What d'you think of that, wor John?

JOHN *is in a corner with the whisky bottle.*

JOHN. Well, to tell you the truth I didn't hear a bloody word.

GEORDIE. C'mon, Vic, get those bottles out… (*To audience.*) Don't worry, you can go for one yourselves in a minute.

The glasses are topped up for the toast to the Union and the song.
NB: the tune is the same as 'It's Only a Story'.

ALL.   Let's drink to the Union, the Union, the Union,
          The Union that's strong as the Tyne and the Wear.
          United we stand but divided we crumble
          And shoulder to shoulder, there's nothing to fear.

          Let's drink to the Union, the Union, the Union,
          The Union that's strong as a good pint of beer.

GEORDIE.   Back there in the bar they've got pints lined up waiting.
          As soon as you've bought them we'll see you back here.

ALL.   So drink to the Union, the Union, the Union.
          As soon as you've bought them, we'll see you back here.

Exeunt omnes, if you'll pardon the expression – with Ad Libs to taste.

ACT TWO

The stage is in darkness.

SONG. Close the coalhouse door, lad,
　　　There's bones inside.
　　　Mangled, splintered piles of bones
　　　Buried 'neath a mile of stones
　　　And not a soul to hear the groans
　　　Close the coalhouse door, lad,
　　　There's bones inside.

A light fades up on THOMAS *as he tells his story.*

THOMAS. The thin seam. You take a lamp, into the most terrifying darkness, and you are not afraid.

And slowly a soft light fades up on THOMAS *and* FRANK, *who is listening. As the story continues, four miners crawl across the the stage, out of and into the darkness, enacting the story. All we see is their lamps.*

THOMAS. You meet a darkness like a velvet pad pressed against your open eye. At two hundred fathoms the sun takes no levy nor gives of his majesty. Only a memory of him and the urge to return quickly.

FRANK. What happened?

THOMAS. First comes the noise.

A dull roar building up.

　　　The noise but no understanding – only the need to escape from the noise, the urge to run but there's no running in the thin seam.

The MEN *trying to get away, speed and urgency without movement, as in a nightmare.*

　　　Only the crawling and tearing and the noise, all of us, me and Jackie, Jimmy and Art, and the noise...

The noise reaches a climax. One of the lamps is extinguished. A loud cry diminishing to silence.

It is finished.

FRANK. Then what?

THOMAS. Then you count heads... one, two, three... no fourth. No Jimmy.

FRANK. Dead?

THOMAS. Caught by the noise.

FRANK. Can you be sure in the dark?

THOMAS. Oh yes. You can be sure. There, in the thin seam, where the roof and the floor meet like the jaws of a vice, there were two hands, the fingers arched so that the nails dug into the dust. You can be sure.

A pause. Then a cross-fade to JOHN *and* RUTH *standing outside the house. Very casual – deliberate contrast to previous sequence – maybe lighting cigarettes, or sharing a bottle of Brown Ale.*

RUTH. Why come out here?

JOHN. The stories.

RUTH. Your grandfather's stories?

JOHN. I've heard them all before.

RUTH. They're marvellous stories.

JOHN. Oh, aye.

RUTH. To somebody like me.

JOHN. I daresay. To somebody like you.

Pause.

RUTH. What's the matter with me?

JOHN. You're a bonny lass, nowt the matter with that.

RUTH. You should be proud of the stories.

JOHN. Stuff them.

RUTH. Why?

33

JOHN. Because, me bonny lass, in the middle of the night when other folks is in bed, I'm off into the pit to earn my bread and butter. I don't need no bloody stories to remind us what it's all about.

Cross-fade to the scene as before. THOMAS *telling the story, and the* MINERS *crouching in the darkness.*

THOMAS. The bare rock is not tender and returns blow for blow with sudden sharpness. The Lord broods over the depths and men disturb his brooding, to pay in passion and the sweat and blood of their bodies.

FRANK. In the thin seam.

THOMAS. Yes. Men do this. My people, your people. They pierce the fabric of his temple; make an incision into the heart of his mystery. At the same time, unthinkingly, they tend the hem of his robe and make most glorious the thin seam of his garment.

Pause.

Then there's a lighting change, as the MINERS *leap up, and become* JACKIE, GEORDIE, MARY *and the* VICAR *and we're back at the party.*

MARY. Get on with the story, man, I want to make a cup of tea.

THOMAS. We kept on crawling for about three days and three nights, till we came out at the colliery at Jawblades...walked all the way back here to Brockenback, just in time for the funeral procession for the lads that didn't get out, like...

FRANK. What did you do?

THOMAS. Why man, we tagged on behind, all in wor dirt, then afterwards we all had a good swill down, then we went out and got blind drunk.

MARY. By, you tell a canny tale, Thomas Milburn.

THOMAS. True, every last word, you ask Jackie.

JACKIE. It's all recorded history.

GEORDIE. I believe you, sure as I'm riding this camel.

FRANK. It's a great story.

THOMAS. If you really think that, fill us up, lad...

34

FRANK. I really think that.

Cross-fade to JOHN *and* RUTH.

JOHN. You look all wrong, don't you?

RUTH. Thank you very much.

JOHN. Standing there, wearing your fancy college scarf, and the slag-heap behind... they divven' match up.

RUTH. Whose fault's that?

JOHN. Always asking questions...

RUTH. Only because I want to know the answers.

JOHN. Ask the right questions. Ask me where's my mam and dad.

RUTH. Where are they?

JOHN. My dad got killed in the pit when I was five... just him on his own, it wasn't what they call a disaster, no headlines, no appeal funds... just him... my mam died of TB couple of years after... one of the great things about pit villages...

RUTH. What?

JOHN. Better chance of dying of rotten lungs than anywhere else in England.

Pause.

RUTH. Actually, I knew about your parents.

JOHN. Did you... actually?

RUTH. Frank told me.

JOHN. Oh, him.

RUTH. What do you mean... oh, him?

JOHN. Well he cleared off, didn't he?

RUTH. And you can't forgive him.

JOHN. I can't forgive him for clearing off. I can't forgive myself for staying.

RUTH. Looks like you can't win.

JOHN. I found that out years ago, pet.

Cross-fade to the party.

FRANK. I think we should have some toasts.

GEORDIE. Never mind the toasts, let's get on with the boozin'...

VICAR. Let us now praise famous men...

GEORDIE. My old mother, she's ninety-six and never used glasses in her life... straight out the bottle...

MARY. They're away now, their feet'll not touch the floor till the morning...

JACKIE. There's only one toast... the Union of workers...

ALL. The Union of workers...

They drink the toast. As they do so, MARY steps forward to sing. RUTH sings the second verse, as a collier's wife.

MARY. My old man's a Union man
As happy as happy can be
He spends his life on a piece-work plan
But it brings no peace to me.
When he comes home at the break of dawn
He gives to me this greetin':

THOMAS. Mary dear, ye've nowt to fear –
I've been to a Union meetin'.

RUTH. My old man's a Union man
As jolly as jolly can be.
He's working now on an overtime ban
But he finds no time for me.
When he comes home tight on a Friday night
He says he's not been cheating
An' he's not been drinkin', oh dear no,
He's been to a Union meeting.

MARY & RUTH. (*Together.*) My old man's a Union man
As bonny as bonny can be
But once in a while he's a family man
And he stays at home wi' me.
And he takes his turns and he minds the bairns
And then he starts repeatin':

THE MEN. Tonight's the night!
Turn out the light!

MARY/RUTH. (*Spoken.*) Ooh, hinnies!
(*Sung.*) That's a lovely Union meeting.

Song ends. Reactions and applause out of which the VICAR's *voice emerges.*

VICAR. If I might break in...

GEORDIE. Aye, gan on, Vic...

VICAR. I'd like to propose another toast...

GEORDIE. And then we'll take a collection for the belfry...

JACKIE. Shut up, man, you're showing your ignorance...

GEORDIE. Well, why shouldn't I? I'm as ignorant as the next man.

VICAR. I'd like to propose a toast to the happy couple, Mr and Mrs Milburn.

ALL. Mr and Mrs Milburn...

VICAR. And that far-off day when they decided to tread the path of matrimony...

MARY. In 1918.

Pause.

THOMAS. 1918.

They drink the toast and a sudden hush.

Music of the time: say 'Keep the Home Fires Burning' on a mouth organ.

THOMAS. Well, you see, in 1918, we'd just had this big war.

MARY. The war to end all wars.

THOMAS. And the country needed lots of coal to fight the war and it turned out the coal owners weren't clever enough to organise it properly... so the Government took over all the mines.

During the following sequence, actors put on hats appropriate to the parts they are playing – cloth caps for the Union of workers, bowlers for the politicians, toppers for the coal owners.

JACKIE. Like nationalisation?

THOMAS. Like nationalisation, aye... and come the end of the war, the coal owners come running to Lloyd George and they say...

37

GEORDIE. Please can we hev wor coal mines back, please?

THOMAS. And Lloyd George says... can ye hell... and then the coal owners say...

GEORDIE. What about wor poor bairns running barefoot in South Kensington?

THOMAS. And Lloyd George says, we'll have a Royal Commission.

Fanfare.

Led by the honourable Mr Sankey... hey, Mr Sankey!

JACKIE as SANKEY.

JACKIE. What is it, David lad?

THOMAS. I'd like ye's to hev a Royal Commission.

JACKIE. Righto. (*To the audience.*) So me and twelve other wise men gans down the pub and we talk it over and then we decided...

JACKIE *has a brief muttered rhubarb chat with three of the cast. He turns to* THOMAS.

We've decided, Mr Lloyd George.

THOMAS. What have ye decided, Mr Sankey?

JACKIE. We think you ought to nationalise the coalmines.

Pause. LLOYD GEORGE *is shaken.*

THOMAS. Now hang on a bit, lad... I'm not sure that's what we wanted you to think... who've you got on your team?

JACKIE. Well, there's three Union men...

The three members don cloth caps and assume social-realist-dignity-of-labour pose.

JACKIE. They want nationalisation.

THOMAS. Well, we cannot trust them... who else?

JACKIE. Well, there's three socialist sympathisers...

The three wave red flags.

They want nationalisation.

THOMAS. Well, we certainly cannot trust them... who else?

38

JACKIE. There's three coal-owners...

The three put on top hats.

They divven' want nationalisation...

THOMAS. Well, I divven' trust them but I dorsen't say so, not out loud...and who else?

JACKIE. Three great industrialists.

The three stick very large cigars in their mouths.

THOMAS. Oh, that's good, you can certainly trust great industrialists.

JACKIE. And they divven' want nationalisation.

THOMAS. Good lads.

JACKIE. So that left me with the casting vote, and I voted in favour.

THOMAS. Ye what?

JACKIE. I voted in favour.

THOMAS. Right, the Royal Commission's against nationalisation.

JACKIE. But it wasn't, it was in favour.

THOMAS. The impartial ones was against it.

JACKIE. Who says great industrialists are impartial?

THOMAS. Me, Lloyd George says it...and you look in the papers in the morning...Believe me, Mr Sankey, I speak as the man whose hand is firmly steering the helm of the ship of state through turbulent waters...

JACKIE. Eee, the fine eloquence of the Welsh!

THOMAS. And another thing, Mr Sankey...

JACKIE. What is it, David lad?

THOMAS. That's the last bloody Royal Commission you get out of me.

JACKIE. Right lads...off you go...

The Royal Commission departs.

GEORDIE *as coal-owner,* JACKIE *as Union man,* THOMAS *as Lloyd George.*

GEORDIE. Please can we have our coal mines back, please?

THOMAS. Yes, you can, if you promise to be good...

GEORDIE. Why, aye, we'll promise to be good.

JACKIE. And that was the first mistake.

THOMAS. And what had you in mind as your first contribution to the national well-being?

GEORDIE. We thought we'd cut the wages of the miners.

THOMAS. So they cut the wages.

JACKIE. And we wouldn't accept the wages cut.

GEORDIE. So we locked them out for three months.

JACKIE. And at the end of three months...we went back to work.

GEORDIE. And we cut their wages.

Fanfare.

FRANK. 1925.

GEORDIE. Stanley Baldwin.

JACKIE. Oh, aye, I remember Stanley Baldwin.

GEORDIE. One of the canniest little fellers you'd never want to meet again.

ALL *as themselves now.*

THOMAS. Hey, and you knaw what happened in 1925.

Fanfare.

ALL. Britain gans back on to the Gold Standard!

Pause.

GEORDIE. Britain gans back onto the Gold Standard?

JACKIE. That's right.

GEORDIE. What the hell does that mean?

VICAR *makes an entrance as ventriloquist, with* FRANK *as the dummy.*

VICAR. Perhaps I can help you there with the assistance of my little friend...

40

JACKIE. Gan on...

VICAR. The Government of 1925 was anxious to maintain the strength of sterling.

GEORDIE. Oh, aye, that's important, we all believe in that, right, lads?

THOMAS. Oh, aye.

JACKIE. Certainly.

VICAR. So the then Chancellor of the Exchequer...Mr Churchill...

Reactions.

GEORDIE. Would that be...Winston S. Churchill?

VICAR. Of course...is something the matter?

JACKIE. The same Winston S. Churchill that sent in the troops against the striking miners in Wales?

VICAR. I'm sorry, I'm only empowered to explain his fiscal policies.

THOMAS. Never mind his fiscal policies. Get on with the pound sterling.

VICAR. The Chancellor thought it right to stabilise the value of the pound...by revaluing it some ten per cent higher than previously.

JOHN *breaks in, as cross talk comedian.*

JOHN. I say, I say, I say. Was this to put the economy back on its feet again?

And now the DUMMY *speaks!*

DUMMY. Exactly.

JOHN. Give the country a fresh chance in world markets?

DUMMY. Precisely.

JOHN. Re-establish our world role?

DUMMY. Absolutely.

JOHN. But I thought you did that by devaluation...by reducing its value, rather than increasing it.

DUMMY. Well...you can, of course, do either...it simply depends... what you believe in.

GEORDIE. By God, it takes a clever dummy to talk rubbish like that.

VICAR. The situation demanded action. (*To* JOHN.) We could use a young chap like you on our side.

JACKIE. But hang on a minute... if you increase the value of the pound...that means the stuff we export is going to cost more...

VICAR. All our exports will cost our customers ten per cent more.

THOMAS. Including coal.

VICAR. Yes, our coal will cost overseas customers ten per cent more.

THOMAS. Aye.

VICAR. Unless.

THOMAS. Unless?

VICAR. Unless we can drastically cut production costs and thus maintain present prices.

THOMAS. And then the coal owners thought of a great way of cutting production costs.

GEORDIE. (*As coal owner.*) We'll cut the miners' wages by ten per cent!

Fanfare.

JACKIE. (*As Union man.*) Ye'll dae nothing of the sort...

DUMMY. The country does rely on the co-operation of all sections of industry in this, our great hour of need... (*To* VICAR.) Saw your lips move.

THOMAS. Oh, hadaway to hell!

Ventriloquist becomes VICAR *again.* DUMMY *reverts to normal, whatever the hell that is.* THOMAS *puts on Stanley Baldwin hat.*

THOMAS. I, Stanley Baldwin, will settle this.

GEORDIE. (*Groucho style.*) The situation is menacing, Stanley.

THOMAS. Aye, it is, lad. But I know what to do about it. We'll hev a Royal Commission!

Fanfare.

JACKIE. And the world breathed again.

MARY *steps forward as Royal Commission.*

THOMAS. Hey, would you mind bein' a Royal Commission?

MARY. Will it take long? I've got a pan of chips on.

THOMAS. Keep it going a bit, hinny, till tempers cool off.

JACKIE *and* GEORDIE – *as Union and Owners – maintain a tense confrontation as* MARY *paces round the floor. One circuit and she returns to* THOMAS.

THOMAS. Well, what hev ye decided?

MARY. Well, we're against nationalisation.

THOMAS. That's grand. And what about cutting wages?

MARY. We're against that.

THOMAS. And what about increasing the hours?

MARY. We're against that. We're against everything really.

THOMAS. And what about the coal owners?

MARY. You can't believe a word they say.

THOMAS. And what about the miners' Union?

MARY. You can believe every word they say.

THOMAS. Good God, that's even worse.

Pause.

Well, that seems like a positive and forward-looking report. Thanks very much, pet.

Gives MARY *a sugar lump and she retreats into the background.*

JACKIE. But we're no further forward.

GEORDIE. What ye ganna dae, Stanley lad?

THOMAS. That's easy. We'll negotiate.

Fanfare.

JACKIE. And the world breathed again.

THOMAS. We'll all get together and hammer out a solution.

THOMAS, JACKIE *and* GEORDIE – *as* BALDWIN, *the Unions and the Owners – link hands and dance round in a circle, ring-a-roses style.* THOMAS *breaks free.*

THOMAS. That settles it, the miners'll have to accept a cut in wages.

JACKIE. Will we hell!

THOMAS. Right, we'll negotiate again.

They dance round again. This time, THOMAS *breaks free, but leaves the other two dancing round.*

THOMAS. What they don't know is that it's May 1926 and I'm ready now...(*To* JACKIE.) Did you say something?

JACKIE. Hey, Stanley. I thought we were negotiating...

THOMAS. We're doing nothing of the sort. You can all gan on strike and to hell with the lot of you!

JACKIE. Right, lads, all out!

Everybody leaves the stage, and the drums beat.

Cross fade to JOHN *and* RUTH.

JOHN. When we were kids, we didn't have Goldilocks and the three bears like the kids in Jesmond...we'd sit on Granda's knee and he'd tell us all about the General Strike...

RUTH. No Cinderella?

JOHN. Nae room for Cinderella or her bloody Prince in Brockenback ...just Arthur Cook and Stanley Baldwin and Will Lawther and Sam Watson...

RUTH. Did you listen to him?

JOHN. Every last word.

RUTH. I've got a friend who's writing a thesis about it...

JOHN. You don't have to write about it...it's built into your brain ...I mean, I can tell you the story, if you're interested...

RUTH. I'm interested...

JOHN. Listening?

RUTH. Every last word.

JOHN. Well...the first thing to know about the General Strike is that my Granda ran it all himself...

RUTH. You mean he was involved in the Strike?

JOHN. Involved? You'd think he's invented it. He was in charge of the pickets in the village.

THOMAS. Right, lads... like I said.

JACKIE *and* GEORDIE *march and counter-march, in a slight parody of the guards outside the Palace, but with strike banners, under* THOMAS'*s direction.*

GEORDIE. What we on the lookout for?

THOMAS. Unauthorised vehicles.

GEORDIE. How do we know which ones is authorised?

THOMAS. You ask me and I tell you.

GEORDIE. I see.

GEORDIE *points to something off-stage.*

GEORDIE. That looks like a vehicle to me.

JACKIE. Is it an armoured car?

THOMAS. Don't be daft, man. It's my Auntie Bella on her tandem.

GEORDIE. They reckon the Government sent fourteen armoured cars to protect a milk cart gannin' from Newcastle to South Shields...

JACKIE. What happened?

GEORDIE. The horse dropped down dead in Gateshead.

JACKIE. Do you wonder?

VICAR *enters as commentator.*

VICAR. 'All our Yesterdays'... an everyday story of country folk ...The General Strike as seen by the newsreel cameras and commentators of the day.

JOHN *does the Pathé News cockerel while the others win Wimbledon, swim the Channel, etc.*

JOHN. Who says the General Strike's a serious business? They certainly don't think so down here where you're watching a charity football match between a police team and a team of strikers...

The two teams run out.

JOHN. And here comes the wife of the Chief Constable to kick off...

MARY *forward*.

FRANK. Where's the ball?

GEORDIE. Never mind the ball, let's get on with the game.

Teams carry off MARY.

JACKIE. The result? Oh, the strikers win by two goals to one... but who cares about the result, the game's the thing... And the hit song of the moment is...

EXPERT. (*Appears singing, Al Jolson style.*) I'm sitting on top of the world...

ALL. (*Off.*) Hadaway to hell.

MARY. Meanwhile the nation marches on gallantly with all the transport in the hands of voluntary labour. In Newcastle upon Tyne, a train steamed into the central station driven by a driver wearing plus fours – you don't see many of those – and missed the platform. A striker, full of typical Geordie humour shouted...

JACKIE. Divven' bother, hinny, you stay where you are – we'll move the platform.

FRANK. And all across England's green and pleasant land, people are flocking to the aid of the country...

VICAR *as Government recruiting officer, approaches* JACKIE.

VICAR. I say, how would you like to flock to the aid of the country?

JACKIE. Why don't you flock yourself?

VICAR. If you become a special constable we'll give you forty-six shillings and thruppence a week, forty-six shillings and thruppence a week... and a house!

JACKIE. Thinks. If I gan back to the pit I'll only get thirty-one shillins' and seven pence farthing a week, and no house.

JACKIE *moves in menacingly*.

VICAR. But you're forgetting something very important.

JACKIE. What?

EXPERT. Everybody's singing... (*Sings.*) I'm sitting on top of the world...

JACKIE *chases him off the stage.*

FRANK. (*Commentator.*) But it isn't all singing at this time of crisis in the land. The Armed Forces are on the alert.

The lads are lined up like an Army squad with GEORDIE *as the* SERGEANT *reading out Churchill's directive.*

GEORDIE. Now then, lads... here's a message specially for you from the Home Secretary...

JACKIE. (*As* SOLDIER.) Is that Winston S, sergeant?

GEORDIE. No. It's Winston S. Churchill, you stupid little man. And what he says is... any action the army has to take to aid the Civil Power will receive the full support of His Majesty's Government...

Pause.

Step forward any man that doesn't understand what that means.

They all step forward.

You horrible lot. What he means is, if you see any strikers causing trouble, it's shoot first and no questions afterwards. Yes, what's the matter with you?

JACKIE. Well, my father and two brothers is on strike. Supposing...

GEORDIE. Oh, you needn't shoot them, just hit them with your rifle butt.

JACKIE. Oh, righto.

GEORDIE. By the left, quick march... (*Sings.*) I'm sitting on top of the world...

They march off, singing the song in chorus.

VICAR. And so throughout the length and breadth of the land people are girding their loins for the struggle to come, urged on by the inspiring words of Rudyard Kipling...

FRANK. Keep ye the law – be swift in all obedience,
Clear the land of evil, drive the road and bridge the ford
Make ye sure to each his own,
That ye reap what ye hath sown,
By the peace among our people, let men know we serve the Lord.

JACKIE. Just a minute...

FRANK. I beg your pardon...

JACKIE. We've got poets on wor side an' all...

FRANK. But this one's been printed in the *British Gazette*, editor, Winston S. Churchill...

JACKIE. And this one's been printed in the Strike newspaper. So your best plan's to hadaway to hell.

Pushes FRANK *away.*

JACKIE. We have fed you all for a hundred years
But that was our doom, you know.
From the time you chained us in the fields
To the strike a week ago
You have eaten our lives, our babies, our wives
But that was our legal share
But if blood be the price of our legal wealth,
Good God we have bought it fair.

Cheers and counter-cheers.

FRANK. (*As commentator.*) Meanwhile the whole world was still singing... (*Sings.*) I'm sitting on top of the world...

VICAR. Wrong, my child.

FRANK. I do beg your pardon, bishop.

VICAR. I'll tell you what the world is singing. (*Sings.*)
Not a penny off the pay
Not a minute on the day.

ALL. Amen.

VICAR. Blessed are the coal owners who make such fair demands.
Blessed are the blacklegs who come from foreign lands.
Blessed are the constables with truncheons in their hands.
And the voice of the miners was heard and the porridge of the nation...

GEORDIE. ...was stirred.

THOMAS *steps forward.*

THOMAS. I, Stanley Baldwin, have an important announcement to make...

A hush.

I, Stanley Baldwin, have resumed negotiations with the TUC. I, Stanley Baldwin, have brought the General Strike to an end, thus preserving democratic government, the Monarchy, the strength of sterling, the Marylebone Cricket Club and I, Stanley Baldwin...

GEORDIE. Goodness me, Stanley, you must be the greatest Prime Minister that ever lived.

THOMAS. I think I must be.

GEORDIE. Altogether now...

ALL. (*Sing.*) I'm sitting on top of the world... (*etc.*)

One final chorus and we're back at the party again.

THOMAS. May 14th the General Strike ended... but the miners stayed out till the October...

MARY. Gluttons for punishment.

THOMAS. Men.

MARY. Who's talking about the men?

JACKIE. I tell my kids how me and my brothers and sisters stayed alive, 'cause of the soup kitchens and they think I'm jokin' ...didn't keep my mother alive, though.

THOMAS. We shouldn't have gone back in the October either.

GEORDIE. Fellers started to gan back, didn't they?

THOMAS. Not in Durham they didn't... solid as a rock... Nottinghamshire and Derbyshire, they went back...

JACKIE. Nothing changes.

THOMAS. They near wrecked the Union...

JACKIE. Like I say, nothing changes.

VICAR. Did you win the strike?

THOMAS. They reduced the wages.

VICAR. You lost?

THOMAS. The miners never won a strike yet. They always win years later. They won the 1831 Strike in 1872. They won the General Strike in 1947.

49

VICAR. To know how to wait is the secret of success?

JACKIE. That's correct thinking, comrade.

MARY. (*To* THOMAS.) They didn't reduce your wages after the General Strike.

THOMAS. That's true.

VICAR. How was that?

MARY. No job, no wages.

THOMAS. I was a lodge official, you see...

FRANK. I thought there was no victimisation...

JACKIE. Thirty-five thousand miners didn't get their jobs back in this county... that's a lot of victimisation.

GEORDIE. Mind you, it was all in the national interest.

JACKIE. Oh aye, that makes you feel a lot warmer inside.

FRANK. Why is it?

Pause.

THOMAS. 'Cause it's the same fellers, that's why...

JACKIE. In 1832...

THOMAS. Lords and landowners...

JACKIE. In 1926...

THOMAS. Lords and landowners...

JACKIE. In 1968...

THOMAS. The Stock Exchange...

GEORDIE. Lords and landowners...

FRANK. They don't own the coalmines...

GEORDIE. They've got the Big Five banks and the jockey club, that's enough... never mind, comes the revolution...

JACKIE. That'll make all the difference.

Music starts. GEORDIE *steps forward for his song. Everybody joins in the chorus.*

GEORDIE. I should have done it yesterday
If I hadn't had a cold
But since I've put this pint away,
I've never felt so bold.

ALL. So as soon as this pub closes,
As soon as this pub closes,
As soon as this pub closes,
The revolution starts.

GEORDIE. I'll shoot the aristocracy
And confiscate their brass
Create a fine democracy
That's truly working class.

ALL. As soon as this pub closes,
As soon as this pub closes,
As soon as this pub closes,
We'll raise the banner high.

GEORDIE. I'll fight the nasty racialists
And scrap the colour bar
Old Enoch and his followers
And every commissar.

ALL. As soon as this pub closes,
As soon as this pub closes,
As soon as this pub closes,
We'll man the barricades.

GEORDIE. So raise your glasses, everyone
For everything is planned
And each and every mother's son
Will see the promised land.

ALL. So as soon as this pub closes,
As soon as this pub closes,
As soon as this pub closes...

GEORDIE. (*Speaks.*) I think I'm goin' to be sick...

He makes a dash for it.

ALL. The revolution comes.

A big, sharp finish and a cross-fade to JOHN *and* RUTH. *Very quiet.*

RUTH. Why do you bother?

JOHN. What do you mean?

RUTH. Digging coal...if it's just been a hundred and fifty years of oppression?

JOHN. 'Cause I don't know any better...a hundred and fifty years, and I don't know any better...I'm like that bloody slag-heap ...built into the landscape...just as solid, just as thick...

RUTH. A bit sad, isn't it?

JOHN. I don't think about it much – it's only people like you makes us think about it.

RUTH. Why not leave?

JOHN. Leave?

RUTH. Leave the pit...leave the village...You're a big strong man.

JOHN. I could get any job at my trade on Teesside, I daresay... engineering, you know, if I fancied it...

RUTH. So when are you going?

JOHN. You're not very bright, are you, for a scholar?

RUTH. Thanks very much...

JOHN. Nae good being upset about it, you're not... There's two old folk in there need someone to look after them like they looked after me...

RUTH. I'm talking about now...your grandparents are part of the past...

JOHN. It's all they've got, isn't it?

RUTH. Yes, but you can't live in the past...the General Strike was forty years ago...

JOHN. It didn't stop with the General Strike – that was just the beginning.

Into Thirties sequence.

THOMAS. 1931.

THOMAS, JACKIE *and* GEORDIE *form a queue.*

THOMAS. 1931, Ramsay Macdonald.

GEORDIE. Jeanette MacDonald.

JACKIE. Charlie Chaplin.

GEORDIE. Oswald Mosley.

JACKIE. Mickey Mouse.

THOMAS. Back to Ramsay Macdonald. Well, lads, what are we ganna dae about this?

JACKIE. Only one thing for it.

GEORDIE. Howay, let's march on Whitehall.

They unfurl 'WE WANT WORK' banner – the band strikes up – maybe a fusion of 'Blaydon Races' and 'The Red Flag' – as they march off the stage and then back again.

MARY *greets them.*

MARY. How did you get on, lads?

JACKIE. Well, he seemed a canny enough fellow that Deputy Assistant Parliamentary Private Secretary.

THOMAS. He didn't dae nothing.

GEORDIE. Ah... but the conscience of the nation was stirred.

Cross-fade to JOHN *and* RUTH.

RUTH. The trouble is, you... all of you, sit around the village, sorry for yourself because you think nobody cares...

JOHN. You reckon someone does care?

RUTH. Of course they do.

JOHN. Name one.

RUTH. I care.

JOHN. What you ganna dae? Start a soup kitchen?

RUTH. That's not what I mean, John. What happens when your grandparents... I mean, they're getting on a bit and...

JOHN. When they die, you mean?

RUTH. Yes.

JOHN. I mean, we just say it – we live with it round here.

RUTH. Would you leave then?

JOHN. You're asking me to think about tomorrow. I never do that. You know why. Like the lads say...you know where you are with the past.

RUTH. On the slag-heap.

JOHN. But at least we know wor place.

Cross-fade to the queue.

THOMAS. 1934. Stanley Baldwin.

JACKIE. Oh, not him again!

THOMAS. Sorry, lads... Stanley Baldwin.

JACKIE. Ye bugger, he's a sticker, I'll say that for him.

THOMAS. Stanley Baldwin.

GEORDIE. Stanley Matthews.

JACKIE. Jessie Matthews.

THOMAS. Greta Garbo.

JACKIE. Mussolini.

GEORDIE. Mickey Mouse.

THOMAS. Stanley Baldwin. Howay, lads.

Marching procedure as before, but this time the music is a little wearier than before – as is the marching.

MARY *greets them on their return.*

MARY. How did it go, lads?

JACKIE. Well, he couldn't see us personally.

GEORDIE. But he seemed canny enough.

MARY. Who?

THOMAS. The office boy.

JACKIE. For an Arsenal supporter, like...

MARY. But nothing's happened...everything's still the same.

GEORDIE. But Mary pet, we stirred the conscience of the nation.

Cross-fade to JOHN *and* RUTH.

JOHN. Bonny, isn't it?

RUTH. Slag-heap by moonlight.

JOHN. Aye. They reckon the NCB's ganna plant grass on it one day and call it part of wor island heritage.

RUTH. They'll maybe do the same for you.

JOHN. They can cover it with icing sugar. Doesn't alter the fact. It's all waste. Along with the whole shooting match. The bands and the banners. The Gala. Singing hymns in Durham Cathedral. It's canny, like. But it's all a confidence trick. When the big boys in London have done with us, they'll chuck us all on the slag heap along with the rest of the waste. They always have and they always will. That's how it works. Dust to dust. Ashes to ashes. And the colliers to the slag-heap.

Cross-fade to the queue as before.

THOMAS. 1937. Neville Chamberlain.

JACKIE. God help us.

GEORDIE. Wee Ellen Wilkinson.

THOMAS. Hughie Gallagher.

JACKIE. Willie Gallagher.

GEORDIE. Patsy Gallagher and Raich Carter and Sunderland won the Cup.

JACKIE. Mind you, it was a long time ago.

GEORDIE. Donald Duck, Mickey Mouse, Pluto...

THOMAS. Neville Chamberlain.

Pause.

THOMAS. Howay, lads.

And off they go with the banner again, as before. As they return, they are joined by FRANK and RUTH, dressed as trendy young things from Woodstock.

MARY. Well, lads, how did it go this time?

JACKIE. I just hope that office cleaner passes the message on, that's all...

GEORDIE. Never mind, the conscience of...you know, I think the nation's forgettin' an' all...

They become uneasily aware of the two young strangers.

THOMAS. Are they with you?

JACKIE. No.

GEORDIE. Never seen them before.

THOMAS. Try an experiment. Right?

They nod.

THOMAS. Neville Chamberlain.

JACKIE. Ellen Wilkinson.

GEORDIE. Hughie Gallagher.

FRANK. Mick Jagger.

RUTH. Marianne Faithfull.

THOMAS. Whyebugger!

Reactions! Shock! Horror! Where did these people come from? And how long are they staying? NB: The style of the song can be adjusted to suit the singers: from Jagger to Dylan to Beatles to Englebert. For now let's assume a bit of basic Geordie rock.

FRANK & RUTH. (*Sing.*) When me father was a lad
  Unemployment was so bad
  He spent best part of his life down at the dole.
  Straight from school to the labour queue
  Raggy clothes and holey shoes
  Combin' pit-heaps for a manky bag o' coal.
  And I'm standin' at the door, at the same old bloody door,
  Waiting for the pay-out as me father did before.

  Nowadays we've got a craze
  To follow clever Keynesian ways
  And computers measure economic growth.
  We've got experts milling round
  Writing theories on the pound
  Caring little whether we can buy a loaf.

By this time everybody else has got the idea and they all join in the chorus, with dancing to match.

ALL. And I'm standin' at the door, at the same old bloody door,
Waiting for the pay-out like me father did before.

FRANK & RUTH. 'Course we didn't like the freeze
But we really tried to please
'Cause we made that little cross to put them in.
Down the river we've been sold
For a pot of cheap Swiss gold
And we're the ones that suffer for their sin.

ALL. And I'm standin' at the door, at the same old bloody door,
Waiting for the pay-out as me father did before.

FRANK and RUTH. Baby, baby, this is true,
I'll be standin' in this queue,
Till the Tyne runs clear and plastic roses sing.
So the next time they come by,
Watch the sky for the custard pie,
And tell 'em straight, it's Charlie Watts for King!

ALL. And I'm standin' at the door, at the same old bloody door,
Waiting for the pay-out like me father did before.

FRANK *leads everybody back into the party, the house, and the present,
with an all-join-in chorus finish and applause into which* JOHN *returns.*

JOHN. Good lad, Frank... I never knew you had it in you...

FRANK. I'm not just a pretty face, you know...

THOMAS. Yes, I really enjoyed that. Not a patch on Bob and Alf
Pearson, mind.

MARY. I always told you he was a good lad... all we can get out
of you is pitman John...

GEORDIE. (*To* JOHN.) Where've you been all night?

JOHN. I was outside with the lass.

JACKIE. They'll have been down the yard.

GEORDIE. Is it a two-seater netty you've got, Tommy?

RUTH. John was showing me our island heritage.

THOMAS. The slag-heap?

JOHN. Naturally. What else is there?

The VICAR *returns but this time fully restored as the* EXPERT.

EXPERT. I'll tell you what else there is. 1939!

THOMAS. 1939. Neville Chamberlain.

GEORDIE. Mickey Mouse.

JACKIE. Pluto.

THOMAS. Neville Chamberlain.

EXPERT. No, no, no... Adolf Hitler... Come along, chaps, seats in all parts.

The men line up and go off, like sheep.

EXPERT. (*As* HITLER.) There will now be an intermission, during which we will march into Poland and fight the Second World War. I therefore order you all to take a twelve-minute interval! Sieg Heil!

He gives the Nazi salute, knocks his hat off and exits. Everybody goes for a drink.

ACT THREE

Out of the darkness:

SONG. Close the coalhouse door, lad,
There's bairns inside.
Bairns that had no time to hide
Bairns that saw the blackness slide
Bairns beneath the mountainside
Close the coalhouse door, lad,
There's bairns inside.

A crashing ecclesiastical chord on an organ and dramatic quasi-religious light on the VICAR *in pulpit pose.*

VICAR. And it came to pass that in the one thousand, nine hundred and forty-seventh year of our Lord, all the earth of the county of Durham did pass into the ownership of the tribes thereof. And the richness of the land did comprise collieries, numbering one hundred and thirty-five, coking plants, numbering sixteen, power stations, numbering eight, brickworks, numbering seventeen, tribal dwellings, numbering twenty-six thousand, fields and vineyards numbering ninety-three thousand acres, and fish and chip shops, numbering one only. And there was weeping and wailing among the rich merchants and moneylenders of the Southern lands, but among the tribes of the North there was great rejoicing. Verily, I say unto you, blessed are the meek, that they shall inherit the earth, and the manifold riches therein.

Cross-fade to GEORDIE, JACKIE *and* MARY, *front of stage, proudly looking at the pithead.*

JACKIE. 1947. Clement Attlee.

GEORDIE. Stafford Cripps.

MARY. Nye Bevan.

GEORDIE. Manny Shinwell.

59

JACKIE. Tomorrow, comrades, this colliery will belong to the people.

MARY. I never thought to see the day of nationalisation.

JACKIE. A Labour Government that believes in Socialism.

GEORDIE. At last, we're ganna taste the fruits of wor labours. Give us a bit tune, eh?

JACKIE *to the piano and they sing*:

MARY. When it's ours, Geordie lad, when it's ours,
There'll be changes, bonny lad, when it's ours.
When the colliers take control,
No more twelve-inch seams of coal,
No more means test, no more dole,

MARY & JACKIE. When it's ours, all ours.

GEORDIE. (*Speaks.*) I saw Manny Shinwell lookin' at Seaham Colliery...

MARY. You saw Manny Shinwell lookin' at Seaham Colliery? What was he sayin'?

GEORDIE. Mine, all mine!
(*Sings.*) When it's ours, Jackie boy, when it's ours,
Man, what glorious times we'll have when it's ours,

JACKIE. What's the future hold for me?

GEORDIE. You can retire at twenty-three!

JACKIE. On full pension?

MARY. Nat'rally!

MARY & JACKIE. When it's ours, all ours.

GEORDIE. (*Speaks.*) So I gans on holiday to the South of France...
and I says to the waiter, 'Hev ye got frogs' legs?'... 'Mais oui,
hinny,' he says...'Right,' I says, 'Hop off and fetch us some
pease pudding.'

MARY. (*Sings.*) When it's ours, Geordie lad, when it's ours,
I've got plans, bonny lad, when it's ours,
Bye, we'll really live it up,
Only best champagne we'll sup,
While Newcastle win the Cup,

MARY & GEORDIE. When it's ours, all ours.

MARY. (*Speaks.*) Did you gan to see Sunderland play on Saturday?

GEORDIE. No...well, they didn't come to see me when I was bad. (*Sings.*) When it's ours, Mary lass, when it's ours,
Mind the wife'll be reet glad when it's ours,

MARY. Tell me Jackie, what's in store?
What will she be grateful for?

GEORDIE. Why, I'll stop in bed wi' hor.

MARY. (*Spoken.*) Eeee!

MARY & GEORDIE. When it's ours, all ours.

GEORDIE. (*Speaks.*) So I says to the gaffer, 'Can I hev the day off work, my wife's expecting a baby'...'Certainly,' he says 'when the baby due?' I says 'Nine months time'.

MARY. (*Sings.*) When it's ours, Geordie lad, when it's ours,
We'll be masters, bonny lad, when it's ours,
(*Ultra posh.*) We may step lightly on the grass.

GEORDIE. (*Ditto.*) To let Lord Londonderry pass.

MARY & GEORDIE. Then we'll kick him up the path,
When it's ours, all ours.

GEORDIE. (*Speaks.*) So Lord Londonderry had this dream. He dreamed he was making an important speech in the House of Lords and when he woke up, he was...

MARY. (*Sings.*) When it's ours, Geordie lad, when it's ours,
There'll be changes, bonny lad, when it's ours.

GEORDIE. (*Doubtful.*) Are ye sure we'll be all right?
Is the future *really* bright?

MARY. (*Speaks.*) Oh, for God's sake, man, Geordie...
(*Sings.*) We *won* this bloody fight,

MARY & GEORDIE. So it's ours, all ours.

Big finish which, with luck, gets a big hand, but music continues for the next verse, which works as a carefully prepared encore.

GEORDIE. When it's ours, Mary lass, when it's ours,
Oh what holidays we'll have, when it's ours.

MARY. California, Santa Fe...

GEORDIE. Winter sports and Saint Tropez...

MARY & GEORDIE. And to hell with Whitley Bay!
When it's ours, all ours.

A big finish and music-hall exit. Fading up lights on the house as JOHN
is getting ready to go on night shift.

JOHN. Good night, Grandma...

MARY. Good night, son.

JOHN. Good night, Granda...

THOMAS. Safe home, lad.

JOHN. Good night. (*General.*)

They all wish JOHN *good night. He indicates he wants a word outside
with* FRANK *and* RUTH.

JOHN. Howay outside, kiddar. (*To* RUTH.) You an' all.

Outside.

FRANK. What's the big secret?

JOHN. She's a good lass, this one.

RUTH. I already knew that.

JOHN. You see? The best yet.

RUTH. How many others have there been?

FRANK. If I told you, you wouldn't believe me.

JOHN. And if I told you, you wouldn't believe me either.

FRANK. But we're grateful for your approval.

JOHN. Except for one thing. She makes you tell the truth.

FRANK. What's wrong with that?

JOHN. You spend half your life underground. There's no time for
debates about the meaning of life when you're on the surface.

RUTH. For a man that isn't interested in the history of the workers,
you've got a lot to say about it...

JOHN. I'm not interested in who built the prison walls or what sort
of bricks they used... but I know the walls are there just the
same...

62

FRANK. It's not a prison. You've got the key. We've all got the key.

JOHN. Lost the key years ago... hole in my pocket.

RUTH. You want to get out, don't you?

JOHN. We all do, if we're honest... we don't talk about it... but you've made me say it out loud... I'm not sure I can forgive you for that. (*Turns to* FRANK.) As for you, kiddar... don't think you've escaped. You might get a train to Newcastle, or London even. You might sail around the world to Australia. You might fly to the Moon. But you never leave a village like Brockenback. It keeps a tight hold and never lets go.

FRANK. That's all right by me.

JOHN. Long as you keep the faith. Good night, kiddar. Good night, bonny lass.

JOHN *moves away into the darkness. They watch him go, then walk us back into the party, where* THOMAS *is in full flow.*

THOMAS. That was a canny enough song but divven' talk to me about nationalisation...

MARY. Ye'll never stop him, now...

JACKIE. What's the matter with it, man? The workers must take over the means of production...

THOMAS. Utopia, they told me, bloody Utopia, and I comes in, first day at work after nationalisation... and what do I see?

MARY. I've heard it all before.

THOMAS. What do I see? The same gaffers.

JACKIE. Don't be daft, man...

THOMAS. The same gaffers, I'm telling ye, there's Alfie Robson standin' there, same as he had done for twenty-odd years... five foot nowt and nasty with it.

JACKIE. Alfie Robson didn't own the pit, he was only the manager ...he wasn't the owner...

GEORDIE. We're all the owners, aren't we? That's what public ownership means. Except when it's a public house. We never own them, do we? We buy them but we never own them.

THOMAS. Who's talking about owners? I'm talking about gaffers. Alfie Robson. And if I was the owner, how come I couldn't sack him?

JACKIE. And I'll tell you something an' all... there's no better record of labour relations anywhere than in the Durham coalfield since nationalisation... twenty years and not one official strike... not one...

THOMAS. And that's another thing.

MARY. I thought it might be.

THOMAS. There's nae decent strikes any more.

JACKIE. That's good, isn't it, nobody really wants strikes.

THOMAS. There's nae fun any more.

MARY. Take no notice of the old fool.

THOMAS. I haven't finished yet.

GEORDIE. Well, hurry up and finish...

THOMAS. What about rationalisation?

JACKIE. The subject on the agenda is nationalisation.

THOMAS. Bugger the agenda, I'm talking about rationalisation.

MARY. I don't know what anybody's talking about.

RUTH. Me neither.

THOMAS. It's nowt to do with women.

MARY. That's not true. We'll have that row after everybody's gone home.

FRANK. What about rationalisation?

THOMAS. And you a scholar...

FRANK. I'm sorry, Granda, I don't see the connection...

THOMAS. The connection is that this village, and this pit, got rationalisation. I mean, the Coal Board says we've got to rationalise the industry...we've got to rationalise Brockenback pit...

Pause.

I mean, they closed the bugger.

Music link, a lighting change and the Labour Exchange door is pushed on again. THOMAS, JACKIE *and* GEORDIE *form a queue.*

THOMAS. 1961. Harold Macmillan.

JACKIE. Huckleberry Hound.

GEORDIE. Yogi Bear.

THOMAS. Harold Macmillan.

Pause.

THOMAS. We're here again, lads. This is what they mean by rationalisation.

JACKIE. Marginal adjustments in the national economy.

GEORDIE. Safeguarding the strength of sterling.

JACKIE. Our world role.

THOMAS. Wor seat at the conference table.

GEORDIE. It still feels like the dole to me.

JACKIE. Only one thing to do.

WILL. Whitehall it'll have to be.

Marching music building up quietly.

GEORDIE. We'll have to stir the conscience of the nation.

The old banners are brought out.

THOMAS. Are you ready, lads?

The music building.

THOMAS. By the left... quick march...

Just as they are about to set off, the EXPERT – *played by the* VICAR *as usual – comes on from the opposite side. He is dressed as a high Cabinet man, and carries a briefcase.*

EXPERT. Don't you go to all that trouble, chaps, we'll come to you.

And he crosses to them. They are stunned.

THOMAS. Ye what?

EXPERT. I am coming to you.

THOMAS. Why, that's a turn-up.

EXPERT. You see, I'm on a fact-finding mission.

JACKIE. What sort of facts do you expect to find?

EXPERT. One can't really say that, till one has, as it were, found them.

He roots around the stage looking for facts.

EXPERT. The point is, gentlemen... chaps... lads...we are very worried about the results of nationalisation and, er... rationalisation, in this area...

THOMAS. So are we.

JACKIE. What are ye ganna dae about it?

EXPERT. We have perfected a new policy... regionalisation!

Fanfare.

THOMAS. Regionalisation?

JACKIE. That sounds grand.

GEORDIE. What is it?

EXPERT. It simply means that from now on, we in Whitehall are determined to take a totally fresh look at you splendid chaps, lads, kiddars, in Durham and Northumberland and...Yorkshire's quite near as well, isn't it?

JACKIE. You mean we'll get a bigger slice of the national cake?

EXPERT. Yes...and very nicely put, if I may say so.

JACKIE. Ta.

THOMAS. But you're all Tories, aren't you?

EXPERT. Well lads, we're all Tories now, unless we're Socialists...

GEORDIE. That's true enough.

EXPERT. My friends...

THOMAS. Watch him...

EXPERT. My friends...we're all brothers in the same family...

THOMAS. Prove it!

EXPERT. I can prove it, friends... because I have brought with me on my fact-finding mission our new secret weapon. Our new symbol of liberty, equality and fraternity.

As the music starts he brings out of his brief case a cloth cap, two sizes too large...and sings...

EXPERT. If you ever go to Tyneside you must watch your P's and Q's
You must learn to say *Newcassel* or their confidence you'll lose.
And in mingling with the common folk you're sure to make a botch,
If you ask for pints of bitter, what you really mean is Scotch,
But there's one thing makes the locals really fall into your lap
Get your picture in the papers with a little cloth cap,
A little cloth cap, a little cloth cap,
You'll make a big impression with a little cloth cap.

You must use the local language when you're talking to the men,
Say a miner is a *pitman* and they'll ask you back again.
And remember when you're in the pub to spit upon the floor,
And if you chew tobacco, well, the compliments will pour.

But there's one thing makes the locals really fall into your lap,
Get your picture in the papers with a little cloth cap;
A little cloth cap, a little cloth cap,
You can eat your singing hinnies from your little cloth cap.

Everybody joins in a final chorus, with a touch of tap or soft shoe to taste.

ALL. A little cloth cap, a little cloth cap,
You can eat your singing hinnies from your little cloth cap.

The EXPERT *makes the song a triumphal procession ending with a big flourishing exit. The men are left feeling quite pleased until they realise they are still standing at the Labour Exchange door.*

THOMAS. Well, it's all very well but I divven' feel any different.

MARY *walks across to them.*

MARY. Is it right they're closing the pit?

THOMAS. That's right.

MARY. If the vicar was here he could say a few suitable words...

GEORDIE. We've already said a few suitable words...

JACKIE. I think the vicar got called away. Typical. There's never a vicar available when you need one.

MARY. What about the little feller in the cap? Has he made any arrangements?

THOMAS. Oh, aye, they're looking after us... me and Jackie here, we're ganna look after the pumps...

GEORDIE. And I'm ganna be redeployed to Datton Colliery... temporarily...

MARY. Temporarily?

JACKIE. Till they build the perfume factory.

MARY. They're going to build a perfume factory here?

GEORDIE. To take up the slack of unemployment...

JACKIE. They're not actually building it yet... they're doing a feasibility study... to see whether it's the right place for a perfume factory.

THOMAS. There's got to be an adequate water supply before you can build a perfume factory.

JACKIE. And proper sewage disposal.

GEORDIE. And the right kind of prevailing winds.

JACKIE. You can't just bash a perfume factory down anywhere.

GEORDIE. Diversification.

MARY. What?

GEORDIE. Diversification... that's what they call it when they close a pit and build a perfume factory...

THOMAS. For God's sake, man, Geordie, we've had nationalisation and rationalisation... and then regionalisation... and now divers-ification... I don't think I can take any more...

GEORDIE. All we lack's constipation.

JACKIE. I've got news for you.

GEORDIE. Oh, I'm sorry... keep taking the tablets...

FRANK *suddenly leaps up from his place in the house, very triumphant.*

FRANK. There's something you're all forgetting.

THOMAS. What's that?

FRANK. The wind of change.

GEORDIE. Stop taking the tablets.

68

MARY. Back to the perfume factory.

FRANK. No, not that at all.

THOMAS. What's he talking about?

FRANK. An eleven percent swing in Gosforth, that's what I'm talking about.

A loud fanfare.

FRANK. 1964. Labour elected!

Fanfare.

During the following sequence, the characters assume positions as follows: GEORDIE, FRANK *and* RUTH *as the three candidates,* JACKIE *as the chairman of television panel consisting of* THOMAS, MARY *and the* VICAR.

Very casual and accidental-looking, slipping back into a party atmosphere at the end without any formal link.

JACKIE. Here is the result for Jesmond Dene South.

GEORDIE. Harry Bradley...

VICAR. (*Quietly.*) Labour...

JACKIE. 26,973...

FRANK. Ernest Gordon-hyphen-Bennett...

VICAR. Conservative...

FRANK. 7,574...

RUTH. Janie Potbender...

VICAR. Liberal...

RUTH. 3,886...

JACKIE. Labour elected... after a recount...

GEORDIE. And I would like to thank my opponents...

FRANK. My constituency workers without whom...

RUTH. And the official Receiver, I mean Returning Officer, for...

GEORDIE. A good...

FRANK. Clean...

RUTH. Fight...

JACKIE. And now for their comments on that result from Jesmond Dene South...

THOMAS. They're all a set of villains, I don't know why you're getting so excited...

MARY. I'm sorry the little Liberal lass lost her deposit, she's a bonny lass...

THOMAS. I bet she lost more than her deposit...

MARY. That'll do, Thomas Milburn...

VICAR. The glory is not in the winning but in the taking part.

MARY. That's not what it says in my Bible.

JACKIE. And for a comment on the swing...

GEORDIE *becomes the swing expert.*

GEORDIE. Well, according to my slide rule and my piece of string, if that swing is repeated throughout the country, Labour will have an overall majority of 1,547.

JACKIE. Wey, you daft devil, there's only just over six hundred seats altogether...

GEORDIE. Well it's an old bit of string, man, Jackie...

JACKIE. And that's a very old joke.

FRANK. It's a great victory, though.

GEORDIE. It certainly is.

JACKIE. Our movement.

And now we're in an election celebration party.

GEORDIE. Aye.

JACKIE. The Labour movement that was made by the miners out of blood, sweat and tears...

ALL. That's right, hear hear...

JACKIE. The men we've stood and cheered as they've spoken from the platform at the Miners' Gala in Durham...

FRANK. A great victory.

GEORDIE. Brothers, we're on our way...

JACKIE. The Labour movement...

They raise their glasses in a toast. THOMAS *hesitates.*

JACKIE. What's the matter, Tommy?

THOMAS. You'll not remember Ramsay Macdonald...

JACKIE. Never mind ancient history, man...I'm giving you a toast ...the Labour movement...

They drink a toast. Glasses down and there is a knock at the door. THOMAS *opens the door. There stands the* EXPERT, *smartly dressed in a Harold Wilson mac, sucking a Harold Wilson pipe.*

EXPERT. I wonder if I might join the party, brothers...

THOMAS. Certainly, come along in...

EXPERT. Thank you, brothers...

He joins them. A glass is thrust into his hands. He drinks with careful robustness.

JACKIE. I don't think we've met, have we?

EXPERT. No, I don't think so...I don't get up this way all that often...not past Huddersfield.

THOMAS. The face is familiar, mind.

EXPERT. Well...perhaps if we say a Government spokesman...

THOMAS. But a loyal member of the Movement?

EXPERT. Goodness, yes, when the Whips are out I'll vote for anything...

GEORDIE. And what was it you wanted?

EXPERT. Well, I've just popped in to explain the Government's fuel policy...

MARY. That's very civil...have a seat, pet.

JACKIE. Just hold hard a minute, brother...is it to do with nationalisation?

EXPERT. Partly, yes.

FRANK. Rationalisation?

EXPERT. That comes into it.

RUTH. Regionalisation?

EXPERT. Oh yes, I'm a firm believer in regionalisation...Dan Smith and the Northern Arts Association and touring outlying areas with popular selections from *Waiting for Godot*. I believe in all of that.

JACKIE. How about...diversification?

EXPERT. I'm glad you asked me that...especially diversification.

JACKIE. Like perfume factories...

EXPERT. Given my own way, perfume factories will spring up like daffodils in March...which brings me to my fuel policy...

THOMAS. Go on...

EXPERT. Anybody heard of nuclear reactors?

GEORDIE. Aye, they dropped one on Hartlepool, just missed the monkey. Did three pounds worth of damage.

EXPERT. Oh no, these are good things, definitely good things.

FRANK. Nuclear reactors?

EXPERT. Nuclear reactors and...

Pause.

High...speed...gas...

He kneels.

ALL. High speed gas?

The EXPERT *gets up.*

JACKIE. Well, we know all about gas, you make it out of coal. Like electricity, you make that out of coal an' all.

EXPERT. How many of you know the North Sea?

JACKIE. The North Sea. Aye, ye can just see it from Whitley Bay...

GEORDIE. I've had many a piddle in there, I mean a paddle.

EXPERT. And what lies beneath the North Sea, full forty fathoms deep?

Pause.

72

GEORDIE. Bird's Eye fish fingers?

EXPERT. High speed gas.

ALL. High speed gas.

EXPERT. Which we shall suck up from the sea-bed in great man-made vacuum cleaners and then blow out over this green and pleasant land as the basis of the first hundred days of my white-hot technological revolution.

JACKIE. High speed... natural gas.

EXPERT. Natural gas... as you so well put it, brother. Armed only with nuclear reactors and high speed gas the nation shall scale the heights...

THOMAS. And what happens to coal?

Pause.

EXPERT. What... happens... to coal.

THOMAS. Aye.

EXPERT. I'm glad you asked me that.

THOMAS. Let's hev an answer, then.

EXPERT. Well, we have a programme in mind... based on a care-fully considered... de-escalation...

JACKIE. Like closing a few more pits?

EXPERT. Rationalise our existing resources.

JACKIE. Like closing a few more pits?

EXPERT. Get our priorities right.

JACKIE. And how are you going to achieve all your aims?

EXPERT. By closing a few more pits...

THOMAS. How many more...

EXPERT. Well, in non-technical language... most of them...

THOMAS. A word with you.

EXPERT. Certainly, brother...

THOMAS. We made your Movement what it is...

EXPERT. Nobody recognises more than us the great debt the Labour movement owes to the miners...

THOMAS. My grandson works at Datton Colliery, and they can produce coal that's cheaper per unit than either high speed gas or high speed nuclear power or high speed pigeon farts...

JACKIE. And production's gone up by sixty percent in the last seven years... that's better than any private industry can claim...

GEORDIE. And the Durham coalfield's running at a profit...

JACKIE. And there hasn't been a serious industrial dispute in twenty years...

THOMAS. Right?

EXPERT. (*Checking his notebook.*) Right...

THOMAS. So you're closing all the pits?

EXPERT. We're taking the broad view...

MARY *moves in.*

MARY. You're not shutting them because it's a terrible job that kills men and makes widows and orphans...

EXPERT. No, it's the white heat of our technology...

MARY. You're not closing them because of the broken backs and silicosis...

EXPERT. We're simply re-assessing our priorities...

MARY. You're not closing them because you want us and our children to have a cleaner, safer, better life...

EXPERT. Not in so many words... I mean, if you consider the National Economy as a big iced cake...

ALL. Oh, hadaway to hell!

Pause.

EXPERT. I do have some good news.

JACKIE. What?

EXPERT. It's full steam ahead on the perfume factory.

They chase him off.

THOMAS. You'll not remember Ramsay Macdonald.

JACKIE. Correction. We'll not forget Ramsay Macdonald.

GEORDIE. But what's the alternative?

MARY. (*At window.*) Here's the alternative coming up the path now.

JACKIE. Ye what?

MARY. The shape of things to come.

Fanfare.

THOMAS. 1972. Edward Heath.

JACKIE. Alec Douglas-Home.

GEORDIE. William Whitelaw.

JACKIE. Reginald Maudling.

GEORDIE. The Comedians!

THOMAS. Edward Heath.

Two quick bars of 'All the Nice Girls Love a Sailor' and the EXPERT *comes on as Sailor Ted.*

GEORDIE. (*To audience as Groucho.*) And this is where the story really starts, folks.

MARY. Have ye dropped in to explain the Government's fuel policy?

TED. Certainly not. We don't believe in policies, as such.

THOMAS. That's a relief.

TED. We believe every lame duck should stand on his good foot.

JACKIE. So what are you after?

TED. Tell me. How many of you have heard of the North Sea?

GEORDIE. Why aye, I've had a piddle in there, I mean a paddle, no, I've said that bit... (*Looks to the others.*) Another bugger on about the North Sea.

TED. And what lies beyond the North Sea full forty thousand leagues?

THOMAS. Beyond?

TED. Beyond.

GEORDIE. Northern Ireland is it?

TED. (*Pained.*) Please...I am referring to no less than Europe.

ALL. Europe?

TED. And on my great white ship, myself at the helm, we shall steer through the foaming breakers into that great dawn that lies ahead, that dawn that will herald our joining hands with our European partners – Beethoven, Wagner, Mozart – in the Promised Land of Tomorrow.

MARY. Why that sounds grand.

WILL. On your great white ship?

TED. Sur mon grand bâteau blanc.

JACKIE. If you're as good as you say you are why don't you just walk across?

FRANK. (*To* THOMAS.) He's got some strange ideas, this one.

THOMAS. You'll not remember Stanley Baldwin.

GEORDIE. And what are we doing while you're steering?

TED. You will be the crew.

JACKIE. If we're ganna be the crew, we'll want a pay rise.

TED. You can have a pay rise.

JACKIE. How much?

TED. N minus one per cent.

JACKIE. That's not enough.

TED. The nation will not be held to ransom. I, Stanley Baldwin, that's to say, Neville Chamberlain, that's to say, Edward Heath...

JACKIE. (*Breaking in.*) I, Joe Gormley, say N minus one per cent is not enough.

TED. I, Edward, said...let there be light, and there was light.

All lights go out. Blackout.

A single candle is lit on stage. Music starts.

ALL. Strike! Strike! Strike! Strike! Strike!

A candle is lit on each word: Strike! Then the song.

FRANK. Strike a match and light a candle.

RUTH. Let it shine, bonny lad...

MARY. Let it shine...

GEORDIE. But not for Jesus.

THOMAS. Let it shine for us, me lad.

ALL. Let it shine, let it shine,
Let it shine, bonny lad,
Strike a match and light a candle
Let it shine, let it shine.

The chorus can be repeated, as more candles are lit.

JACKIE. (*Speaking.*) You know, I'm getting a bit sick of lighting candles. I've got another idea.

He sings.

JACKIE. Strike a match and light the fuses,
Let it burn, bonny lad,
Let it burn but not for Jesus,
Let it burn for us, me lad,

ALL. Let it burn, let it burn,
Let it burn, bonny lad.
Strike a match and light the fuses,
Let it burn, let it burn.

The music continues under as the lights go on. They look around but SAILOR TED *has gone.*

THOMAS. Hang on a minute, Jackie lad...you're singing about revolution.

JACKIE. Why aye, I'm singing about revolution. Is it a revolution ye want?

GEORDIE. I'd have done it yesterday, if I hadn't had a cold.

THOMAS. Maybes if I was a bit younger...

Pause.

And at least I wouldn't be scared of winning!

GEORDIE. But howay man Tommy, it couldn't happen here.

Music continues and carries us into the song 'It Couldn't Happen Here'. A chorus song with individuals singing the verses. Loud and robust and angry.

ALL. It couldn't happen here, no, it couldn't happen here,
We've made a little Eden so it couldn't happen here.

GEORDIE. We need no revolution to achieve the things we've planned,
No fighting in the streets for us, we've got the promised land.

ALL. So it couldn't happen here, no, it couldn't happen here,
No fighting in the streets for us, so it couldn't happen here.

VICAR. There are no more injustices in this dear island home,
Equality, Fraternity and Liberty are won.

ALL. So it couldn't happen here, no, it couldn't happen here,
There are no more injustices, so it couldn't happen here.

MARY. There are no idle rich men now who profit from the poor,
There are no landed gentry shooting grouse upon the moor.

ALL. So it couldn't happen here, no it couldn't happen here,
There are no landed gentry, so it couldn't happen here.

FRANK. There is no exploitation so why should we try to change,
For no one's making thousands playing on the Stock Exchange.

ALL. So it couldn't happen here, no, it couldn't happen here,
For no one's making thousands so it couldn't happen here.

JACKIE. And even in adversity we share an equal role,
Just witness all the stockbrokers a-waiting at the dole.

ALL. So it couldn't happen here, no, it couldn't happen here,
Just witness all the stockbrokers, so it couldn't happen here.

RUTH. There are no wicked landlords here who charge excessive rent,
Our peasants own the land, you see, that's why they're quite content.

ALL. So it couldn't happen here, no, it couldn't happen here,
Our peasants own the land, you see, so it couldn't happen here.

THOMAS. There are no chinless wonders making love on silken sheets,
There are no people living rough and begging on the streets.

ALL. So it couldn't happen here, no, it couldn't happen here,
There are no people begging so it couldn't happen here.

There are no royal palaces with a thousand empty rooms,
There are no people forced to live in dirty stinking slums.

So it couldn't happen here, no, it couldn't happen here,
There are no royal palaces so it couldn't happen here.

A big loud finish. Out of it emerges a knocking at the door.

MARY. There's somebody at the door.

THOMAS. You're hearing things, woman.

MARY. I'm telling you there is...

JACKIE. Counter-revolutionary neighbours, complaining about the noise.

The knocking continues. There's a slow realisation of what it might mean.

MARY. I'll go.

MARY *goes to the door. She greets* HUGHIE – *the pit messenger.*

HUGHIE. Mrs Milburn.

MARY. You know it is...

HUGHIE. Your grandson John works at the pit...

MARY. I know he does...

HUGHIE. There's been an accident.

RUTH. No...

THOMAS. Quiet!

MARY. What sort of accident?

HUGHIE. A fall of stone... John was working with his maintenance gang... on the face... we don't know exactly where they are... just the other side... no contact, you see...

Silent reactions.

HUGHIE. As soon as there's any more news.

MARY. Yes.

HUGHIE. Other calls to make.

MARY. Yes.

HUGHIE *goes out. No conversation. Just quiet music playing, perhaps a guitar or mouth-organ. Into the following sequence which is played, hard and simply, in a very domestic context of tea-making and drinking – the normal crisis reaction.*

MARY. There might be something on the news.

FRANK. (*As Radio One announcer.*) News is coming in of an accident at Datton Colliery in... County Durham. There are no further details as yet. Meanwhile, in the West End, the age of Aquarius has dawned with the opening of the musical *Hair*...

A little quote from 'The Age of Aquarius' merging into our main theme. Then THOMAS *speaks.*

THOMAS. He walks about like a god, afraid of no one. If he feels like working, he works. Nobody can hold the big whip over him. It doesn't exist. Sometimes he's got a lot of money, sometimes he's broke to the wide. He likes to gamble with his money. Sometimes he wins; occasionally he doesn't. Inside his particular prison he possesses liberty. My lad, dour, hard as the rock he tunnels, contradictory and uncertain to understand unless you know the way the cleat of his nature runs. But this is the way they are made; the way they have to be.

Music link.

FRANK. (*As announcer.*) Latest news of the pit disaster. Eight men are trapped behind a fall of rock and rescue teams are hard at work. Meanwhile, in sport, the controversy over Basil D'Oliveira continues.

Music link.

VICAR. Come unto me, all ye men that labour and are heavy laden, and I will give you rest. Take my yoke unto you and learn of me; for I am meek and lowly in heart; and ye shall find rest unto your souls. For my yoke is easy and my burden is light.

JACKIE. Lucky you.

Music link.

FRANK. (*As announcer.*) There is no more news of the accident at Datton Colliery. Rescue teams are at work. Meanwhile, in the Top Twenty, Louis Armstrong celebrates twenty-nine weeks in the charts. Like the man says...What A Wonderful World.

A little touch of Louis fading to music link.

JACKIE. He works in order to live. What he produces for himself is not the silk that he weaves, not the gold that he draws from the mines, not the palace that he builds. What he produces for himself is wages, and silk, gold, palaces resolve themselves into the means of subsistence...a cotton jacket, some copper coins, and a lodging... And the worker...does he consider his weaving, spinning, drilling, turning, building, shovelling, stone breaking as a manifestation of his life, as life? On the contrary, life begins for him when this activity ends...He does not even reckon labour as part of his life, it is rather a sacrifice of his life.

Music link.

FRANK. (*As announcer.*) And it's closing down time from your Radio Wonderful station, good night, everybody, and if you're still up, having a party, celebrating some great family occasion, well, have yourselves a swinging time, so good night, stay bright and it's yours truly saying 'bye for now.

The first bars of National Anthem, abruptly switched off. Then a silence and a waiting. Everybody self-consciously drinking tea, trying and failing to think of anything to say. Till the pithead bell rings.

JACKIE. Who's that?

THOMAS. There's naebody down there.

And they realise. They all dash to the pithead and THOMAS *sets the winding gear going. The cage appears and out of it steps* JOHN *in pit-gear, helmet, black face.*

MARY. John...

JOHN. Who did you think? The bloody Black and White minstrel show?

THOMAS. What happened, lad?

JOHN. I remembered your story...I just kept on walking till I came to the old shaft...and here I am, well, ye divven' like to miss a party...

Hugs and kisses all round.

JACKIE *and* GEORDIE *step forward, very casual and conversational but apart from the main group.*

GEORDIE. I like a happy ending, don't you?

JACKIE. Ye cannot beat it.

GEORDIE. What happened next? Do you remember?

JACKIE. John got hisself a job in engineering...

GEORDIE. What? On the mighty Teesside conurbation?

JACKIE. The other two went back to Jesmond and got on with their postgraduate researches...

GEORDIE. Dirty beasts...

JACKIE. Eh?

GEORDIE. Young married couple... he says to her, do you fancy half an hour on the rug... no, she says... oh dear, he says, we'll never get that rug finished...

JACKIE. Anyhow, it was all a long time ago.

GEORDIE. 1968.

JACKIE. Half a lifetime.

GEORDIE. Doesn't the time fly when you're being shafted by White-hall?

Now the rest of the company, apart from JOHN, *drift downstage, joining* JACKIE *and* GEORDIE *in the present day.*

MARY. The 1980s.

THOMAS. I remember the 1980s like it was yesterday.

MARY. And we know what a bloody awful day it was yesterday.

FRANK. The 1980s.

THOMAS. Margaret Thatcher.

VICAR. Rupert Murdoch.

RUTH. Roland Rat.

THOMAS. Margaret Thatcher.

GEORDIE. And another bloody strike.

JACKIE. The longest ever.

THOMAS. And the best ever. Because it wasn't about money.

GEORDIE. But we lost, didn't we?

JACKIE. It's still too early to say.

MARY. But that's another story for another day. And when it's told, it'll be the women telling it.

JACKIE. Anyhow, it's only a story...

GEORDIE. Is it?

JACKIE. The whole shooting match. Actors dressed up.

GEORDIE. Getaway.

JACKIE. They'll be down the Job Centre like the rest of us when this job's finished. Look at them.

And they're all together in the queue outside the Job Centre.

GEORDIE. I never knew that...maybes they could march on White-hall, stir the conscience of the nation...

JACKIE. Maybe they will.

GEORDIE. I'll tell you somethin', Jackie, though...

JACKIE. What?

GEORDIE. You say it's only a story...

JACKIE. Aye.

GEORDIE. It's a canny old story...

A chorus song, addressed to the audience. The verses hard and bitter. The choruses jolly. During the song, the stage is filled with the whole cast, the band in uniform, lodge banners, portraits of the great men: Tommy Hepburn, Martin Jude, Tommy Burt, William Crawford and Sam Watson. Till at the end the stage is full of gutsy movement and hard colour.

ALL. It's only a story, a story, a story,
    It's only a story, a fanciful tale,
    Just ask the rich pitmen who live in Westminster,
    It's only a story, a fanciful tale.

JACKIE. There's no need to weep and there's no need to moan
    So wipe out the memories and tek yourself home.

ALL. It's only a story, a story, a story,
It's only a story, a fanciful tale,
Just ask the rich pitmen who live in Westminster,
It's only a story, a fanciful tale.

GEORDIE. And nobody suffered and nobody died
And no one went hungry and no widows cried.

ALL. It's only a story, a story, a story,
It's only a story, a fanciful tale,
Just ask the rich pitmen who live in Westminster,
It's only a story, a fanciful tale.

THOMAS. There were no strikes or lock-outs, no gas in the seam
No, none of it happened, it's all a bad dream.

ALL. It's only a story, a story, a story,
It's only a story, a fanciful tale,
Just ask the rich pitmen who live in Westminster,
It's only a story, a fanciful tale.

So off you go home to your bright cosy fire
Throw a shovel more coal on the funeral pyre.

It's only a story, a story, a story,
It's only a story, a fanciful tale,
Just ask the rich pitmen who live in Westminster,
It's only a story, a fanciful tale.

And the music continues, more quietly, and changing the tune, as JOHN
moves forward, still in his pit-helmet and gear.

JOHN. (*Sings, unaccompanied.*)
Close the coalhouse door, lad,
The Tory way
On the slag-heap we've been hoyed
And Maggie Thatcher's overjoyed
Another million unemployed
Close the coalhouse door, lad
The Major way

Close the coalhouse door, lad
And stay outside
Geordie's crawled out of his hole
Geordie's standing at the dole
Geordie's paid the price of coal
So close the coalhouse door, lad

There's blood inside,
There's bones inside,
There's bairns inside,
So stay...outside.

A silence, a pause, then everybody turns quickly towards the pithead.
They bow their heads in homage.

A fade to blackout.

SONGS BY ALEX GLASGOW

Song p. 9

Close the coalhouse door, lad, / There's blood inside. Blood from broken hands and feet / Blood that's dried on pit-black meat Blood from hearts that know no beat Close the coalhouse door, lad, / There's blood inside.

Each verse is a preface to a separate Act. That is, the second verse opens the second Act and the third verse opens the third Act. The fourth verse, however, is set at the very end of the play as a coda to the final song, and is written out in full on page 84.

Song p. 18

When that I was and a little tiny boy, Me daddy said to me, 'The time has come, me bonny bonny bairn, To learn your A B C.' Now Daddy was a Lodge Chairman In the coalfields of the Tyne And that A B C was different From the Enid Blyton kind. He sang:

A is for Alienation that made me the man that I am and B's for the boss who's a bastard, a bourgeois who don't give a damn.

All the alphabet couplets C/D, E/F, etc up to U/V are as above in the repeated section.

W is for all willing workers and that's where the memory fades for X Y and Z, me dear daddy said, will be written on the street barricades. And now that I'm not a

90

Eb   Bb   Eb   Bb   Eb

little tiny boy Me daddy says to me, 'Please try to forget the

Ab   Eb   Bb   Eb   Bb

things I said, Especially the A B C.' For Daddy's no longer a

Eb   Ab   Eb   Bb   Ab

Union man And he's had to change his plea. His alphabet is

Eb   Bb   Eb

different now Since they made him a Labour M.P.

Song p. 23

a mi   G

Time for to make a stand, me lads, Time for to take a

a mi   G

hand, me lads, Time for us to unite, me lads, Time for to start a

a mi   C   d mi   a mi

fight, me lads. Time, Time, Time, Time for to get the

G   a mi

pitman some justice and peace——

91

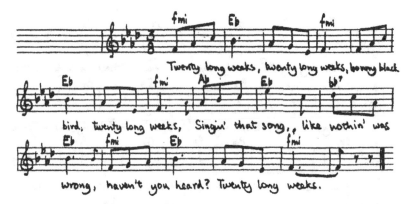

Both second and third verses are accompanied by the men singing 'Time' very softly as a counterpoint.

Song p. 26

Song p. 28   Each clause of the Miners' Regulations Bill is punctuated by a line from 'Time'.

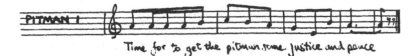

PITMAN I

Time for to get the pitman some justice and peace

Song p. 31

Let's drink to the Union, the Union, the

Union, The Union that's strong as a good pint of beer. Down-

stairs in the bar they've got pints lined up waiting. As soon as you've

supped them we'll see you back here. So drink to the

Union, the Union, the Union, As soon as you've

supped them, we'll see you back here.

Song p. 36

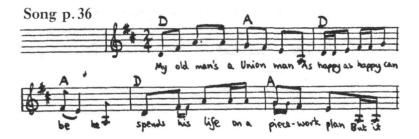

My old man's a Union man As happy as happy can

be be spends his life on a piece-work plan But it

brings no peace to me. When he comes home at the

break of dawn He gives to me this greetin':

Mary dear, ye've nowt to fear—I've been to a Union

meetin'.

Song p. 48

Not a penny off the pay Not a

minute on the day. A - men. Blessed

are the coal owners who make such fair demands.

Blessed are the blacklegs who come from foreign lands.

Blessed are the constables with truncheons in their hands.

A — men And the voice of the miners was heard and the

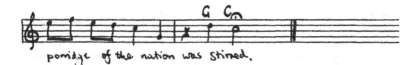

porridge of the nation was stirred.

Song p. 51

I should have done it yesterday If I hadn't had a cold But since I've put this pint away, I've never felt so bold. So as soon as this pub closes, As soon as this pub closes, As soon as this pub closes, The revolution starts.

Song p. 56

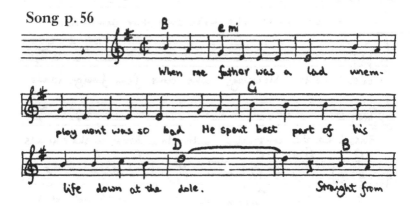

When me father was a lad unemployment was so bad He spent best part of his life down at the dole. Straight from

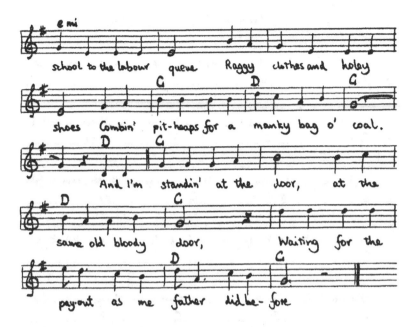

e mi

school to the labour queue Raggy clothes and holey

G D G

shoes Combin' pit-heaps for a manky bag o' coal.

D G

And I'm standin' at the door, at the

D C

same old bloody door, Waiting for the

D C

pay-out as me father did be-fore

Song p. 60

C F

When it's ours, Geordie lad, when it's

C G (spoken)

ours, There'll be changes, bonny lad, when it's ours. When

C C7 F D7

us colliers take control, No more twelve-inch seams of coal, No more

C G C F C

means-test, no more dole, When it's ours, all ours.

(spoken) F   d mi

If you ever go to Tyneside you must

Bb   C   d mi   G

watch your P's and Q's, You must learn to say Newcassel or their

C7   C   A7   d mi

confidence you'll lose. And in mingling with the common folk

B7   d mi   C   d mi

you're sure to make a botch If you ask for pints of bitter, What you

C7   C   F

really want is Scotch. But there's one thing makes the

d mi   Bb   C   F

locals really fall into your lap Get your picture in the

C   F   Bb

papers with a little cloth cap; A little cloth

F   Bb   F

cap, a little cloth cap, You'll make a big im-

C   F

pression with a little cloth cap.

Song p. 77

Strike a match and light the fu-ses,

Let it burn, bonny lad, Let it burn but

not for Jesus Let it burn for us, me lad.

Let it burn, let it burn, Let it burn,

bonny lad Strike a match and light the fuses

let it burn, let it burn.

Song p. 78

Song p. 79

Song p. 83

It's only a story, a story, a story, It's only a story, a fanciful tale, Just ask the rich pitmen that live here in Jesmond, It's only a story, a fanciful tale. There's no need to weep and there's no need to moan So wipe out the memories and tak yourself home.

At the end of the final chorus, modulate to C sharp minor for the fourth verse of 'Close the Coalhouse Door'.

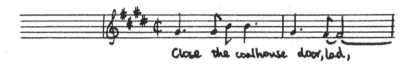

Close the coalhouse door, lad,

There's blood inside.

Geordie's standing at the dole, and Mrs Jackson,

like a fool, Complains about the price of coal.

Close the coalhouse door, lad

there's blood inside, there's

bones inside, There's bairns inside,

So stay outside